THE FORBIDDEN DIARY

Other McGraw-Hill Military/History Aviation Titles

THE FORBIDDEN DIARY

A B-24 Navigator Remembers

John L. Stewart

McGraw-Hill
New York   San Francisco   Washington, D.C.   Auckland
Bogotá   Caracas   Lisbon   London   Madrid   Mexico City
Milan   Montreal   New Delhi   San Juan   Singapore
Sydney   Tokyo   Toronto

Library of Congress Cataloging-in-Publication Data

Stewart, John Lawrence.
    The forbidden diary : a B-24 navigator remembers / John L.
  Stewart.
        p.   cm.
      ISBN 0-07-158187-1
      1. Stewart, John Lawrence.   2. World War, 1939-1945—Aerial
  operations, American.   3. World War, 1939-1945—Campaigns—Europe.
  4. World War, 1939-1945—Personal narratives, American.   5. United
  States.   Army Air Forces—Biography.   6. Flight navigators—United
  States—Biography.   I. Title.
  D790.S8887   1998
  940.54'4973—dc21   97-44417
                                                                      CIP

McGraw-Hill

A Division of The McGraw·Hill Companies

1 2 3 4 5 6 7 8 9 0   DOC/DOC   9 0 2 1 0 9 8 7

ISBN 0-07-158187-1

*The sponsoring editor for this book was Shelley Carr, the editing
supervisor was Bernard Onken, and the production supervisor was
Sherri Souffrance. It was set in Fairfield by Michele Bettermann and
Kim Sheran of McGraw-Hill's Professional Book Group composition
unit, Hightstown, N.J.*

Printed and bound by R. R. Donnelley & Sons Company.

McGraw-Hill books are available at special quantity discounts to use
as premiums and sales promotions, or for use in corporate training
programs. For more information, please write to the Director of
Special Sales, McGraw-Hill, 11 West 19th Street, New York, NY
10011. Or contact your local bookstore.

This book is printed on recycled, acid-free paper containing a minimum of 50% recycled, de-inked fiber.

CONTENTS

CHAPTER 6: INTERLUDE   65

CHAPTER 7: TWO MORE AND A VACATION   89

CHAPTER 8: GERMAN WEAPONS AND MORE MISSIONS   103

CHAPTER 9: MORE MISSIONS   117

THE BEGINNING

INTRODUCTION

It is now the spring of 1997. Over 52 years ago I was in England. My job was to navigate a B-24 Liberator bomber over Germany and other European points of interest. Unlike many, I kept a secret written record of the exploits of myself and my crew. What is presented here is drawn largely from this written record. Unlike other crew members, I also retained photocopies of mission air routes and other tangible evidence of premission briefings.

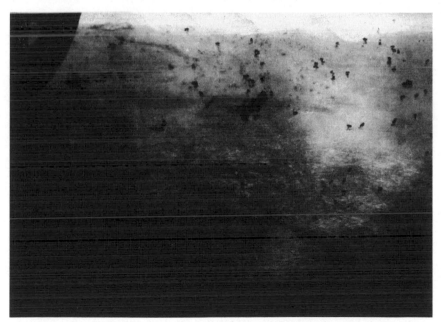

FIGURE 1-1. Flak over Berlin. Picture taken from waist of author's plane.

FIGURE 1-2. Bombs away in southern Germany. Alps in background. Author can be seen in side window behind nose turret.

Ours was neither an outstanding nor an underachieving crew. Just average. We were luckier than most, completing our missions without suffering injuries. Occasionally we did receive some aircraft damage, but it never kept us from getting back home. For the most part we made it through without serious psychological scars, albeit it is difficult to know if some of us carried wounds into later life.

We were part of the 467th Bomb Group, 789th Squadron. Our plane was the *Gremlin Manor,* and we had a pretty lady in a swimsuit painted on our flight jackets. The emblem never was affixed to our bomber. Every time we or someone else took it out, it would return with flak damage, which kept it in repair. For the most part, we had to fly other people's airplanes. But that was OK because maintenance of all aircraft was quite satisfactory.

At takeoff, our plane weighed up to 72,000 pounds, including 2700 gallons of gasoline and 8000 pounds of bombs. The crew of 10 included 4 officers (pilot, copilot, navigator, and bombardier) and 6 enlisted men: nose, tail, 2 waist gunners, an engineer/top turret gunner, and a radio operator. The belly turret was removed from most of the B-24 bombers of the 8th Air Force. By today's standards, our ship was pretty small.

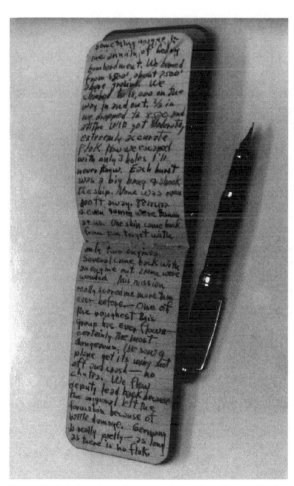

FIGURE 1-3. Sample page from the diary of missions.

"RACKHEATH AGGIES"

467TH BOMBARDMENT GROUP

FIGURE 1-4.   Insignia of the 467th Bomb Group.

789TH BOMBARDMENT SQUADRON

"THE FLYING BOXCAR"

FIGURE 1-5.   Insignia of the 789th Bomb Squadron.

FIGURE 1-6.   Nose art for the *Gremlin Manor.*

The gross weight of the Boeing 747 can be over 10 times as much. But the B-24 seemed big to us.

Most of the time we flew at altitudes in the range of 18,000 to 24,000 feet. The B-17s above us used to call us their "bottom flak cover." We were a little faster and carried more bombs than the 17s. It is claimed that our engines were better than theirs. We could fly deeper into Europe than could the 17s, which prolonged our exposure to enemy action and thus turned out to be a mixed blessing to air crew members.

My "office" was in the nose section, between the front gun turret and the rudder pedals of the pilots. I stood backward, hunched over a desk to which maps had to be tacked. Leakage of air around the gun turret would otherwise blow maps around. When we were over enemy territory, we each wore a flak vest and steel helmet. Other items of attire for the well-dressed aviator included a heated flight suit, boots, and gloves. And we all prayed a bit that the heating system

FIGURE 1-7. Complete flying outfit with oxygen mask. Add flak suit and helmet when over Germany.

would continue to work in the often 40 degrees below zero environment. We wore a 45 pistol in a shoulder holster and a parachute harness. We carried a little waterproof package containing a map of Europe and a saw. This kit was supposed to "guarantee" that we could escape if we should have to bail out over enemy territory. My parachute had to be clipped on to the harness in order to be used. In all of my flying, I don't recall being able to sit down on a decent seat. On occasion, however, I could rest on one of the large cartridge cases that fed the twin caliber-50 machine guns in the nose turret.

When the bombardier did his thing, I would have to straddle him as he crouched over the Nordon bombsight. This instrument was a beautiful example of high technology without the digital computer that people of today might presume to be an absolute necessity. It was gyrostabilized, and, when on the bomb run, it completely controlled the aircraft. My drift meter was also clever, with its gyrostabilization. When in formation, all

FIGURE 1-8. Cloth map and saw escape kit.

FIGURE 1-9. The original crew. *Back row, left to right:* Lt. John Belingheri, pilot; Lt. Vernon O. Mason, copilot; Lt. James E. Wisner, bombardier; and Lt. John L. Stewart, navigator. *Front row, left to right:* Cpl. Thermon Winfield, engineer and waist gunner; Cpl. Herbert Leighty, upper gunner; Cpl. Albert Buchman, radio operator; Cpl. Roy Chastain, tail gunner; Cpl. Roy C. Page, armor and waist gunner; and Sgt. Philmore Zilbert, nose gunner.

aircraft would drop their bombs on a cue from the lead plane. If we were not acting as a lead plane, we usually did not carry a bombardier. It was up to the nose gunner or me to do the honors, triggering the intervelometer to lay down a string of explosions at prescribed intervals along the ground. If we got separated from the group, then I would try to be the bombardier as well, pretending to know all about the Nordon gadget.

Actually, the bombardier had little or nothing to do except when on the bomb run. One of these specialists was reported to check out two or three flak suits and create a little tent, doubly reinforced at his bottom. When ready for bombing, he would crawl out, do his job, and immediately crawl back in.

Our bomb group had a nasty reputation for an almost excessive amount of work in practice flying. But it paid off in award after award for precision bombing. Our tight formations were probably partly responsible for our not experiencing serious attacks from German fighters. Why? Imagine yourself on an attacking pursuit curve. If the formation you are attacking is tight, you would confront 15 or more caliber-50 machine guns, all going at once. Unfortunately, practice does not come cheap. We lost 33, killed in ferrying and practice, 19 in practice over England alone.

Our bomb group had another reputation. My wife, Rita, is from England, but I met her in the USA years after the war, in 1951. When I told her I was at Rackheath, she recalled (with some horror) that we were noted far and wide as a group with wild and crazy parties. My wife was a bit young for fraternizing with the likes of us. It was her older sisters that recounted our crazy exploits. Perhaps our reputation came in part from our illustrious leader, Col. "Black Al" Shower.

Before I joined the group, it had chalked up over 100 missions. A few weeks after we invaded the continent, the group stopped flying combat and ferried gasoline to France. The return from France involved "rum running" (actually, Cognac). Perhaps this helped grow our reputation as well. I suspect that our group was secretly honored more than any other for the liquid gold it brought back to air force headquarters!

Compared to our counterparts in Africa and Asia, we were lucky because we could socialize and drink beer between missions. There was, however, an effective means for controlling beer drinking. That is, when one spent more time in the "gents' room" than at the bar, it was time to back off (just a bit). We all had bikes to go to the local pubs in quaint English villages. Or to go to the "Muscle Palace" for dancing and fraternizing in the city of Norwich. It is probable that fighting these other battles helped to maintain sensibilities in truly stressful situations where life depended upon the speed and direction of a piece of flak.

PERSONAL INFORMATION

Before launching into a blow-by-blow account of my air force experience (back then it was "the Army Air Corps"), a brief account of my premilitary life will be forced upon the reader. I was born and raised in Pasadena, California, except for 2 years when I lived in San Francisco during the time of the San Francisco World's Fair and the building of the bridges. I was a radio hobbyist "ham" operator, an amateur telescope maker, a pretty good badminton player, a so-so football player, a not-so-good violinist, and an occasional gymnast. Almost all boys of that era were Boy Scouts, and many were also members of the YMCA. The YMCA was preferred because it had the best swimming pool in the area. I learned to smoke and drink and function as a buss boy and later a waiter at the prestigious and opulent Huntington Hotel under the tutelage of head waiter Pierre Gonzales. (We were always curious about his name because he presented himself as having come from France.) I was 17 or 18 (well after Boy Scout and YMCA memberships). On occasion I stood in for the bull fiddle player so he could dance with the customers (at least certain "favored" ones).

In those days, college-bound students took algebra and trigonometry and physics in high school. I started college preengineering in early 1943, turning 18 in April. Being young and foolish, I wanted to fly and so signed up to be an aviation cadet. Actually, signing up was not entirely voluntary because the alternative was to be drafted and sent out as a rifleman. Active duty started in June, shortly after the end of spring term. Testing programs sought to determine whether one was qualified to be an airman officer and, if so, which one. My testing did not actually occur until some months after I started my service career. It turned out that I qualified for all three, but I selected navigator. I reasoned that analytical skills would be better retained with this specialty, which would ease reentry to college after it was all over. (No young person ever thinks that life might end in a war.) My logic turned out to be correct. Had I selected pilot training, I never would have gone overseas, let alone seen combat (unless it turned out to be over North Korea). Shortages of navigators resulted in a speedup of training. I reached England only a few months past the age of 19 as a second lieutenant and completed all my missions shortly after I turned 20 as a first lieutenant. I was one of the youngest officers in the group.

What else do I remember about the war prior to entering service? I recall standing on heights north of Pasadena (Altadena) and watching a barrage along the coast some 30 miles away. In those days, there was not much smog in the Los Angeles basin. (The clear night air brought hoards of people to Southern California, which then ended the era of good visibility.) People certainly acted foolishly, running about like a bunch of ants whose nest had been disturbed. Logistically, the spread-out nature of our area would never have enticed the Japanese to undertake much bombing, let alone an invasion. Was the barrage for publicity reasons or just a matter of hysteria?

I remember something else early in 1942. Our junior high school (which went through the tenth grade) was well integrated with Latinos, blacks, and Asians. I played football as a right guard. The backfield consisted entirely of African Americans. We were color blind. And we were very disturbed when our Japanese American friends were taken away—true Americans! They were good and motivated students who were born in this country, and many knew only English as a mother tongue. This shame has lasted to the present. The late Senator Hayakawa from California considered the relocation program to be a blessing in disguise because it forced many Japanese Americans out of their ethnic compounds to become fully integrated into the American culture. Perhaps he was right.

Note on the school system: California had (has?) a rather unorthodox system. Elementary school through the sixth grade was followed by junior high school through the tenth grade, which is normally halfway through a conventional high school program. Then there was a 4-year program at a junior college consisting of the last 2 years of high school and the first 2 years of college. It was called the "6-4-4 plan." One of its disadvantages was that it did not lead to formation of lasting friendships through high school reunions because the last 2 years gathered students from all the junior high schools in the area into one large campus. But it did emphasize the importance of high school math and science because of the close relationship with college-level courses, and it encouraged students to continue beyond the high school level.

When I attended Pasadena Junior College, one of the students was an exceptional football player (not baseball) and was generally admired as a local hero. It was Jackie Robinson.

Like many well-meaning citizens, my father was a block warden, white steel helmet and all. I think he wanted to join up, but he was a bit too old. He volunteered for the Army Air Corps in World War I and went to England as a wing repairer. He admitted to me that he had never even seen a wing before. The American Expeditionary Force (AEF) had two old machines, but only one flew and towed targets for training. My father flew as an "observer" who held the tow rope. He held the rank of a staff sergeant. The second machine was used for parts. He never got to France, but he did describe the zeppelin raids on London. Maybe his experiences were responsible for my desire to enlist in the air corps instead of the navy. So much for World War I except to say that my father and his friends considered their war to be the really big one.

For many years, my father sold White Rock products throughout California. Their soda water was about the only product that made bathtub gin and whisky drinkable during the 1920s and early 1930s. White Rock was the producer of Sarsaparilla, used as a soft drink during Wild West times. But the company downsized (familiar term today?) and later disappeared due to competition from companies having more sophisticated marketing methods. My father was suddenly out of work while I was away at my foreign job. This unemployment didn't last long because he had many friends in the grocery distribution business. He turned to selling rum. After the war, he sold jams and preserves for a very good Chicago company and had considerable success.

My mother was at one time a kindergarten teacher and also a short story writer with some selling success in the 1920s and 1930s. However, family responsibilities hampered writing with output declining in the 1940s. I still have a bunch of her short story manuscripts that I might one day try to get published.

Both of my parents were born in California in the 1890s. Both of my mother's parents were doctors. But they could not get along because one loved San Francisco and the other was wedded to Pasadena.

I was born in 1925 during prohibition, and I grew up in the 1930s during the great depression. I recall seeing old cars driving through, mattresses on top, just as in *Grapes of Wrath* and other now classic books. Because Dad's products sold so well with illegal booze and the products had little or no competition, we did not suffer much from the depression. In fact, we usually had maids or other household help. Maids were paid about 30 dollars per month plus room and board. The maid's night out was usually Thursday. I do recall that, as I grew into my teenage years, the maids seemed to be getting older. Did my parents have a reason for this? We lived in rented houses for part of the period because of moves between Southern and Northern California. What would now sell for perhaps a million dollars rented at the time for about $60 per month.

I do remember an interesting thing about the prohibition and postprohibition eras. There was always a large 10-gallon crock under the sink that was filled with smelly stuff. It was beer. Hardly an uncommon find in many households. I didn't get any of it.

Not many of us experience a moment of national fame or notoriety. My father did have one such time in the sun about a year after the war ended. There was a serious fire at the La Salle Hotel in Chicago (June, 1946). The newspaper story title was "Two Sleep On Despite Warnings to Flee Fire." My father even got his picture in the paper. I quote:

> John P. Stewart of Pasadena, Calif., West Coast representative for a Chicago canning firm, was less nonchalant. "I had just gone to bed shortly after midnight," he said, "when someone came slamming on my door." He was in Room 1237, he said. "I thought it was some drunks, so I called to them to let me alone. Then I dropped off to sleep." At 4 A.M., with the fire out, more "drunks" came to his door and broke it down. Stewart admitted he was "mad as the devil"—until he realized they were firemen.

So, you see, my family is famous!

TRAINING

PRENAVIGATION

I graduated from high school in February, 1943, and immediately began a college preparatory program (science and engineering) at Pasadena Junior College. (The "junior" has since become "community.") In April, about the time of my eighteenth birthday, I signed up for aviation cadet training. I was allowed to complete my first college-level semester. Somewhat frightened and bewildered, I left home by train in June, 1943.

My uncle Howard Finley was a newspaper photographer. He started me out with the classical "short-snorter bill." Currency from visited countries would be taped together in a long string with various associates, friends, and others signing their names. The first bit of money, was, of course, a one-dollar bill.

The first stop was Kearns, Utah, for basic training. We did everything peculiar to the infantry and nothing even remotely suggesting aviation. This ordeal lasted 6 weeks. Most of us showed evidence of a "serious disease" in the form of raw tail bones. The cause was interminable periods of sit-ups on the rocky parade ground. None of us got out to do mischief, so there is not much to tell about for this phase of the training other than 5:00 A.M. inspections, meals, calisthenics, and 9:00 or 10:00 P.M. bedtimes.

One interesting experience at Kearns was "sniffing." No, not glue. Rather, it was of mustard gas, phosgene, and other such things associated with "illegal" forms of warfare. The objective was to give us the ability to recognize a toxic gas if we were subjected to one.

Our next stop was a 9-week stay at Jamestown College in Jamestown, North Dakota. Fortunately, it was summertime. A winter visit there for a Southern Californian might not have been negotiated! We studied such things as history, trigonometry, physics, sanitation, military courtesy, civil air regulations, and so on.

I recall that this was the first place where we had the opportunity to escape the compound and have a night on the town. After one wild night out, I recall my bunk mate in the upper bunk climbed down and, hanging on the edge of the bunk, let go with everything. I emphasize "everything." A group of us was reprimanded for our drunken conduct, and we were required to walk a few "tours" as punishment. What is a "tour"? It is an hour or two at a time in full dress with rifle, marching back and forth. It can get pretty hot in North Dakota in the summer!

The fun part at Jamestown was flight training. We each got 10 hours of dual instruction in a little 45- to 55-horsepower Piper Cub. The field was grass. The planes had no brakes. And

FIGURE 2-1.   Air view of Jamestown College.

they were all "tail draggers." Lots of Piper Cubs are still flying, but most now have bigger engines (to the extraordinary number of 65 horsepower) and brakes. This was my first experience ever with a control stick.

When it was time to leave Jamestown for my next assignment, a problem arose. I was in the hospital. I don't remember if the diagnosis was German measles or nasal pharyngitis. I pleaded with the hospital personnel and all the good saints to put me on the train with my classmates, which they did. Maybe they were glad to get rid of an embarrassing holdover!

The real clearinghouse was my next assignment at the Santa Ana, California, army preflight school. Here we continued with topics introduced at Jamestown plus such subjects as map reading and other things that had something to do with flying. We were subjected to a barrage of weird and complicated tests relating to physical coordination and psychological evaluations. From all this, most of us were categorized as being suited for one or more of three positions, namely, pilot, navigator, or bombardier. The few that didn't make the grade went on to other schools not involving flying or perhaps were given the opportunity to become enlisted crew members such as gunners. I qualified for all three, but chose the navigation category because of my interest in calculating things, which would help me in continuing my education after the mess was over.

At Santa Ana, I once got to visit with my parents and brother. They traveled from Pasadena for the visit, using some precious gasoline according to their A-card rationing allotment. But contact was through a fence. Maybe they thought we might run away and join the navy! By then, I was lean and had very short hair. I think this bothered them: "Poor boy."

We did have an interesting experience at Santa Ana. We were put into a pressure chamber and subjected to the equivalent of high-altitude flying without oxygen. The etiology of the experience as one goes up is first a sense of euphoria and well-being, then sleepiness, then unconsciousness. Our test did not go this far. Writing with pen or pencil as one ascends clearly shows how one's capabilities deteriorate with altitude.

EFFECT OF OXYGEN-WANT ON
HANDWRITING DURING ASCENT

ASCENT TO 25,000 FEET WITHOUT OXYGEN	EXPLANATORY REMARKS
A sample of normal hand-writing in flight at 2000 ft	Control specimen of normal handwriting.
10000 ft - breathless	No apparent effect.
15000 ft - feel uneasy generally punch feeling some numbness in legs and hands	Beginning muscular incoordination.
1800 ft ...	Definite physical and mental inefficiency.
3000 ft - faint - numbness in legs - vision fading	Last zero off both 18,000 and 20,000—marked incoordination.
22000 ft pail or rod lastble pale to me feel better	Feeling better? Evidence of false feeling of well-being.
23000 ft feel good except for my feathing or both legs numbness	Feel good. Insight, judgment and coordination very faulty.
24000 feet — ...	Mental and physical helplessness.
25000 ft ax ygen turned on	Improvement with few breaths of oxygen.
3000 ft. they look brighter - Hearing returns feel o.k. now -	Last zero left off—general improvement, but not completely normal.

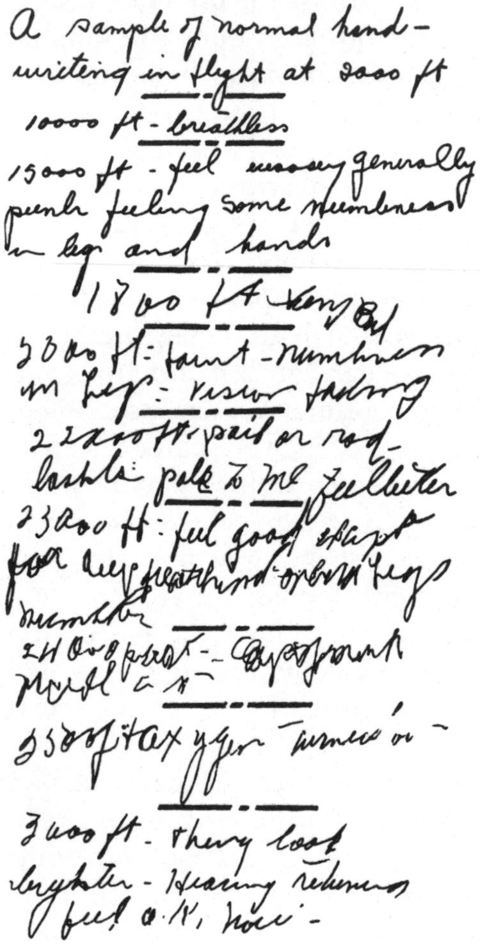

FIGURE 2-2.   Effect of oxygen-want on ascent to 25,000 feet.

Navigators and bombardiers are occasionally required to replace a gunner if the gunner is incapacitated from wounds or worse. We were required to have some ability with machine guns and to operate turrets containing twin caliber-50 machine guns from aircraft in flight. This requirement sent me to Kingman Air Field, Arizona. We learned on the ground and in the air. The aircraft were B-17s, and the targets were anything on the ground that moved. Good thing the large area was off-limits to everyone and everything (except possibly coyotes). Part of the area was Frenchman's Flats, which later became famous in connection with the atom bomb. One or two subjects at Kingman got to be a bit sophisticated, such as the concept of the feedback control system on the electric nose turret on the B-17. The one we used on the B-24 was hydraulic.

But there was more. We had to learn to strip and reassemble caliber-50 machine guns while wearing thick gloves. Some ground training was fun with pistols and carbines and submachine guns. We also had fun with skeet shooting, which was to help us to estimate lead on a moving target. This turned out to be valuable training where gunners shot at conventional aircraft on standard pursuit curves. But it did not help to discourage German jet aircraft from flythrough attacks late in the war. Many of us later realized that, had the Germans been able to build and fuel more jet aircraft, our program of daylight bombing could not have continued.

FIGURE 2-3.   The A-14 demand oxygen mask.

FIGURE 2-4.   Firing a 50-caliber machine gun at Kingman.

I got my first pair of wings at Kingman, those of an aviation gunner. Most of us also got a couple of medals because we were able to show that we could hit the side of a barn with and without closed eyes.

We didn't do much partying at Kingman. First, it is some distance from anything exciting. And second, there was not a lot of free time available. So we just sat around and enjoyed shooting at things whenever the opportunity presented itself. We had to curtail our animal instincts.

SOME TOOLS OF THE TRADE

The final phase of my formal training to become an aerial navigator took place at an air base in Hondo, Texas. Hondo is located in West Texas, sometimes referred to as "God's wasteland." It was possible to have a night on the town in San Antonio, about an hour away by bus. We could visit the Alamo and various and sundry bars and bistros. But we didn't partake of such frivolities too often. I must admit that I, and most of my teenage comrades, maximized our opportunities for undertaking disgraceful behavior. No one seemed particularly upset with these antics. I guess it was realized that it might be our last hurrah! I do recall one incident. Roads were lined with ditches to control water during periods of heavy rain. After getting off the bus returning from San Antonio, I suddenly realized that, for some reason that remains a mystery, I was walking waist deep in one of these ditches.

In February, 1944, I began training at Hondo. Along with the usual daybreak or earlier wakeup, calisthenics, and other military stuff, we spent much of the time in accelerated classroom settings, plus something on the order of 100 hours flight time. We flew in the twin Beach C-45. There were three of us in the cabin, each with a desk, drift meter, and top bubble where we used our bubble sextants for sun and star "shots" and checked headings with an astrocompass. Each of us had a handy window for doing pilotage (albeit, West Texas doesn't have much to look at).

The basic task of the navigator is to maintain constant allegiance to the *dead-reckoning* (or DR) *method* of navigation. I will say more about DR in Appendix A for those that want to get into some of the details. Maps are prepared as *mercator projections*, which often show no ground features at all. In fact, we often constructed our own coordinate system maps from plain paper. The navigator would mark latitude and longitude values appropriate to the flight. Important points along a flight path were also marked in latitude and longitude. One degree of latitude is a distance of 60 nautical miles (about 69 statute miles). A degree is separated into 60 *minutes* such that 1 minute is 1 nautical mile in latitude. These numbers apply to longitude at the equator but somewhat less at the latitude of Hondo (eventually decreasing to zero distance per degree of longitude at the north or south pole).

The dead-reckoning process cannot be ignored for even a short time in an aircraft moving at 4 miles per minute (albeit, the C-45 flew at less than half this speed). If disregarded so that position became questionable, one could get lost. Then the only salvation would be to get a fix. A *fix* can be derived from features on the ground or from various electronic means or from the stars. More than once in combat where all electronic navigation aids were (usually) jammed, with the ground obscured by clouds or fog, I would have to depend on DR for literally hours at a time. In trying to locate myself over Berlin, I once actually shot a sun line. This gives a line along which you are located, but not a fix. Better than nothing!

The tools of DR besides charts were the venerable E-6B "computer," a divider, a plotter, the airspeed meter, altimeter, and the magnetic compass. If the ground (or sea water surface) could be seen, the drift meter could find the difference between true heading and course over the ground. It could also be used to get ground speed by timing motion between two lines in the drift meter view of the ground. In this way, the wind aloft could be determined, which is vital to accurate DR. If the air was bumpy, the compass and drift meter could become difficult to read and errors could accumulate. If the pilot wandered in heading, the navigator tended to go a little crazy trying to keep up with him. A major assist to the DR method was the gyrostabilized drift meter, which I used in combat but not in school. The gyrostabilized flux gate compass was another godsend but not all aircraft were equipped with this, and none in school.

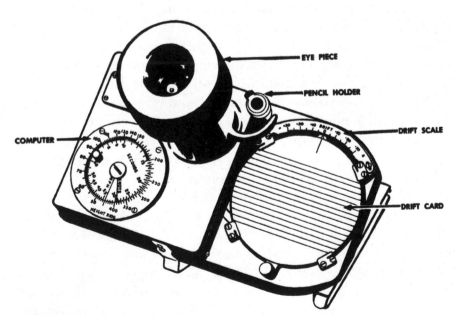

FIGURE 2-5. B-5 drift meter (nongyro).

FAIRCHILD TYPE A-10

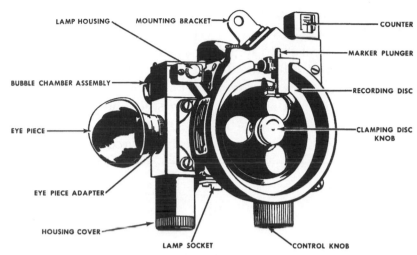

LAMP HOUSING   MOUNTING BRACKET   COUNTER

MARKER PLUNGER

BUBBLE CHAMBER ASSEMBLY   RECORDING DISC

EYE PIECE   CLAMPING DISC KNOB

EYE PIECE ADAPTER

HOUSING COVER

LAMP SOCKET   CONTROL KNOB

FIGURE 2-6.   The A-10 bubble sextant.

In training, we used a large magnetic compass similar to those found on boats. A compass cover, similar to the cover for a round cake, protected the device when it was not in use. These covers had a second application as an alternative to a sick sack. Lots of us gave up breakfast or lunch to the compass cover. We had to look at tiny details on maps while the airplane bumped along. For a time, few of us had yet acquired the equivalent of sea legs. But we eventually did.

We were required to learn locations of planets and stars so that we could "shoot" them with a bubble sextant. If there was a partial cloud cover, we had to be quick to identify and shoot them. Knowing the time was important because a 4-second error could result in a one-mile error. We did not have electronic watches. Only wind up ones. Even today's most inexpensive watches are more accurate. Being able to shoot stars and the sun is what really distinguishes the navigator from all other crew members. Only he can do this, or the somewhat similar task of getting true heading with an astrocompass.

But we did get useful training of an academic kind, which, at least for me, paid off in speeding my reentry to civilian life as an electrical engineering student. I guess I did pretty well in navigation school. Although no academic awards were issued, I did get asked if I was willing to stay on as an instructor. Being young and foolish, all I wanted to do was to get into the action. Perhaps some historian or psychologist might find a study of postwar crew members of interest. Did different specialists tend to follow different kinds of careers? I suspect that we navigators were the nerds of the Army Air Corps.

There is more that needs to be said about our tools and methods. But I will defer that to Appendix A to avoid the danger of boring those who are more interested in the trials and tribulations of a flyboy in war.

GETTING OVER THERE

THE TRIP

Our class of navigators graduated in July, 1944. Most of us received commissions as second lieutenants and thus became "officers and gentlemen" (where I use the second term advisedly). I was all of 19 years old. We could now replace our gunner's wings with those of the navigator.

From Hondo, we went to Pueblo, Colorado, via Lincoln, Nebraska, for a bit of R&R (rest and rehabilitation). My aunt was a short story writer with some degree of success selling to magazines. She belonged to a group of writers, one of whom lived in Lincoln. I looked up her friend whose regular employment was running a boarding house for young working women. You can imagine my interest upon discovering this! Unfortunately, excessive supervision and such things led to total frustration. I am reminded of a joke about a man in heaven who descends to visit an old friend who went the other way. The reader may recall the story.

At Pueblo we were assembled into individual crews that remained together "until death do us part." Our craft was the B-24, which was produced in greater volume than any other bomber. It flew faster and carried a bigger bomb load than the only other heavy bomber in Europe, the B-17. But it did not fly quite as high. We did not have the much larger and heavier B-29 in Europe; they were all in the Pacific.

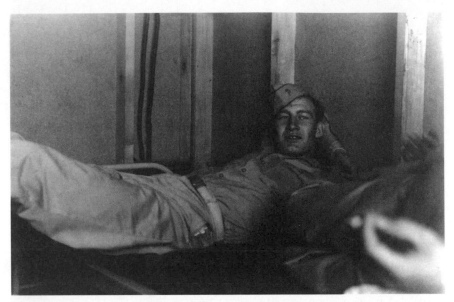

FIGURE 3-1.   John Belingheri relaxing at Pueblo, Colorado.

FIGURE 3-2.   Art on walls of room at Pueblo.

Armament consisted of three turrets, each with a pair of caliber-50 machine guns, nose, upper, and tail. The ball turret was not installed in Europe (although I did have some fun rotating about in these in gunnery school). There were also two individual caliber-50 guns, which the waist gunners handled through large open windows, one on each side. Pressurization was something we did not even know existed!

My crew had been practicing together for several weeks before I arrived. There was a persistent shortage of navigators. I trained with the group for only 4 weeks before we got our orders to go overseas. Up to the last, we really did not know just where "overseas" would be.

From Pueblo, we made a brief visit to Topeka, Kansas, for some more R&R. We did get to go out on the town in Topeka. This time drinking became subordinate to chasing, with some good times experienced. Our copilot, Vernon Mason, and I began to pal around on such jaunts. He was all of one or two years older than I and had been married. He was from Houston with a favorite toast: "Here's to Houston, little city by the sea, where a whisky glass and a woman's ass made a horse's ass out of me." I have long wondered if this poem somehow relates to his short marriage!

We next journeyed to Camp Kilmer, New Jersey, where there was less partying. Then finally, we were off to somewhere in a most insulting manner—by boat. The ship was the *Thomas H. Barry*, sister ship of the *Morrow Castle*. It was about 600 feet long and about as wide. Before the war it was one of the more or less luxurious means of travel for the international set. In recent years, we had learned of the enormously heavy losses of oceangoing vessels of all kinds, primarily sunk by German submarines and surface cruisers. Maybe it was a blessing not to be told how bad the situation really was. We were a bit like sitting ducks, all crowded together in our water bed motel. On one occasion, we observed depth charges exploding off our beam. Were we being stalked?

The principal pastime was playing hearts. We did have some booze. But this was a mixed blessing for some of us. I got sick from a little too much of it and spent the next few days in misery with seasickness. But I can't blame it all on the whisky because most of us did not feel all that well. Other features of the voyage included saltwater showers with saltwater soap. The food was at least acceptable. There were a lot of us on board. We slept in bunks stacked three or four high. I can't remember which.

We docked at Southampton harbor November 1, 1944, and left for Stone, England, where we would be assigned to a bomb group.

RACKHEATH

We were assigned to the 467th Bomb Group, 789th Bomb Squadron. I have wondered all these years how such big numbers ever came about. Does this mean that we had 500 or more bomb groups in the USA, with each one having the better part of a thousand squadrons? Maybe the numbers were to honor Senator this or that. Who knows!

Our airfield was in East Anglia on the estate of Sir Edward Stacey. This is a beautiful part of England, green and lush. I now live in a place that is not too different (including lots of rain), namely, the west side of the Cascade mountains of Washington state, across the river from Portland, Oregon. Unlike me, our pilot, Lt. Belingheri, did not like the area very much, primarily because of the lousy flying weather. Maybe his upbringing in the high desert of Nevada had something to do with his preferences. From the point of view of a pilot, however, the weather indeed was crummy.

The 467th came to England shortly before D-Day. The first mission they flew was on April 10, 1944. At that time, many missions went to France. For some time after D-Day, tactical targets in France continued to be pounded until General Bradley was able to break out of the Normandy invasion area.

The group went off operations on September 11, in order to truck gasoline to the advancing American forces in France. They did not return to combat operations and strategic bombing until

FIGURE 3-3.   Oblique view of Rackheath airport area.

FIGURE 3-4.   Sir Edward Stacey's cottage.

FIGURE 3-5.   Sir Edward Stacey's pond.

FIGURE 3-6.   The estate from the back side.

FIGURE 3-7.   Some of our Nissan huts.

October 3. They had trucked (by air) well over a half million gallons of gasoline to France. Return flights brought cognac (and garter belts) back. Tactical bombing resumed on October 16. Some who were there at the time observed that the short period of combat inactivity resulted in reduced efficiency and bombing effectiveness. With (hated) practice missions, this problem was soon overcome and the group regained its premier status in terms of bombing accuracy.

I arrived at Rackheath on November 7, 1944, along with the complete crew. The town is about 3 miles northeast of Norwich. Ground school, training, and practice missions filled most of our time. I learned how to use the *G box*, a marvelous aid to navigation, something like loran but at ultrahigh frequencies and capable of a fix in one step. It was a British development. *History:* An Englishman by the name of R. J. Dippy is the acknowledged father of the *GEE navigation system.* The idea was born before World War II. The first name G came about because it was defined as a *grid navigation system.* People prefer words to letters, and so G became *GEE* in England. But we kept using the single letter.

Losses for this field prior to my presence since the arrival of the 467th in England were only a bit over 1 percent per mission. As time went on, losses became more severe. But

FIGURE 3-8. The invasion coast shortly after D-Day.

FIGURE 3-9.   Bombed marshalling yard at Orlean, France, shortly after D-Day.

even 1 percent is large. After a tour of some 30 missions, statistics say you are almost one-third dead.

The maximum (normal) effort of a single bomb group for a combat mission was 4 squadrons of 9 planes each for a total of 36 aircraft. A more typical effort used 3 squadrons, but sometimes the group sent out only 1 or 2 squadrons, or perhaps split a multisquadron effort among different targets. An all-out effort, as was mounted on Christmas Eve, 1944, got over 50 of our aircraft to the target, flying war-weary planes including our unarmed B-24 which was normally used to help assemble formations.

The 8th Air Force had three divisions, two with B-17 Flying Fortresses, and one with B-24 Liberators. A number of fighter groups were part of the 8th, their mission being to escort us over enemy territory as protection against German fighters. Each division was made up of 3 or 4 combat wings.

Each wing contained several bomb groups with each bomb group having 3 or 4 squadrons of 9 aircraft each. Our second air division had a total of 14 bomb groups along with 5 fighter squadrons.

You can do some arithmetic to determine numbers. At 36 planes per bomb group and 14 groups, a division has 504. Now include the B-17s for two more divisions, and you get almost 1500 planes that can attack targets in Germany on the same day. At 10 men per plane, an all-out effort would thus involve some 15,000 human targets. The press back home would sometimes refer to "thousand-plane raids." The numbers are correct, maybe even conservative. On Christmas Eve, the numbers could have been half again as large. Then add twin-engine bombers (not part of the 8th) along with the British air force and various fighter and attack aircraft. Pretty awesome!

Note: The heavies of the 15th Air Force in the Mediterranean theater were all B-24 bombers. Their exploits remain famous for the bombing of the Ploesti oil fields. After capturing part of Italy, bombers of the 15th could bomb targets in southern Germany and Austria, crossing the Alps both ways in order to do so. Lots of B-24s were used in the Pacific theater as well where their long-range capabilities were important. There also was a navy version, which had only one large centered vertical tail. It was used for patrol and submarine hunting.

On November 21, my pilot went on his first mission with an experienced crew. In this way he could gain valuable information as to what combat was like. The mission was to bomb an oil refinery at Hamberg (and adjacent Harburg). Flak was intense. None of our group's planes was lost, but some were badly damaged. One lost instruments, hydraulic system, and flaps, and its number 2 engine was on fire. Our pilot's plane had a couple of holes in it, but nothing too serious. In his memoirs, John Belingheri comments: "It was the first time I had seen enemy lines and the flak was heavy that day over the target. I knew all the crew members were scared so I didn't feel too bad because I was scared too."

A bit of history may be of interest here. Throughout the war in Europe, we lost a lot of airmen. I don't know the exact number, but I have read and/or heard of numbers in the range of 20,000 to 200,000. The number killed in the 8th Air Force probably totals somewhat over 20,000 with many thousands more wounded or missing. Our second division alone counts 7000 killed in action. The larger number may include losses by our allies as well as our own and may also include wounded and missing. These statistics are frightening in retrospect. The occupation of being an 8th Air Force crew member might qualify as the most dangerous wartime trade of any in the entire U.S. military system. I don't know if the numbers include losses in training and accidents not related to enemy action. As near as I can recall, it was in the range of 5 percent.

Before continuing, let me say something about our bomb group and its leadership by Col. Al Shower. He was a stickler on training. We did more of this than any other bomb group. But it paid off. Our formations were tight, which served to discourage attacks by German fighters. With a tight formation, a pursuit plane flying a normal pursuit curve would confront a squadron with 15 to as many as 40 caliber-50 machine guns all firing at once. Some of the bullets were tracers with the light pointing forward, which no doubt made the fighter pilots somewhat nervous. But more, our group consistently received highest honors in bombing accuracy.

BAPTISM BY FIRE

FIRST MISSION

I am somewhat motivated to sing: "This is number one and the fun has just begun...." My first mission was on December 2, 1944. The target was a railroad marshalling yard in Bingen, Germany. We often went to such tactical (non-strategic) targets in order to hamper the enemy's ability to supply their troops opposing our advances in France. This trip was later called a "milk run" because we received little flak. There was a great deal of this stuff at a safe distance and a few puffs perhaps 100 yards off of our wing. You can imagine the concern of a wide-eyed kid trying to keep track of the route. Definition of *milk run*: a mission without "significant" enemy action or navigational difficulties (such as running out of fuel).

Before saying more about the mission itself, some details relating to organization and tactics must be described. A better understanding of procedures in this and subsequent missions will then be assured.

Getting "knocked up" (a British term for getting awakened) was almost always well before dawn. Remember that this was England at a latitude further north than any part of the lower 48 states. It was winter and not too far away in time from the winter solstice. So dawn came late and nightfall came early.

The premission breakfast was always good, including eggs and bacon or sausage, cereal, juice, fruit, and bread and rolls.

The philosophy might have been a little like that applied to the last meal of a convict about to be executed. No Spam for breakfast! This was saved for dinner, along with brussels sprouts, brussels sprouts, and brussels sprouts.

Our pilot, John Belingheri, observed that, although one got real eggs when scheduled for a mission, the fare was powdered eggs otherwise. Those on a mission were awakened very early, maybe 2 A.M., with breakfast shortly thereafter. When not on a mission, wake-up was around 6 A.M. John liked real eggs but not the dried variety. He had a standing request that, if either of the other two crews in our hut was to fly that day and our crew was not, then they would awaken him so he could also get the good breakfast. Then he would go back to bed! I guess I am a bit different. Getting to sleep longer is almost worth having to eat Spam (or worse) for breakfast!

After breakfast came briefing. The joint briefing was for everyone. The general route was outlined, the target was described, and possible problems from flak and fighters were revealed. After this briefing, the enlisted crew members went to the aircraft in order to make it ready for flight. One of the enlisted men was the engineer who was knowledgeable in such matters with some airframe and engine (A&E) mechanics training.

The officers went to their specialized briefings, pilot and copilot to one, bombardier to another (if the mission called for a separate bombardier), and we navigators to ours. We received detailed navigation information and best guesses on weather and winds aloft. Weather was obviously of great importance to the success of a mission, and the navigator was the official weather officer on each aircraft. Flak areas were shown so we would know what should be avoided, along with alternate targets and emergency landing fields. We also got information on bombs, bomb release settings, and the Nordon bomb sight, especially if we were not scheduled as a lead plane or alternate. If not a lead plane, we would bomb by toggling on the lead plane's release, which was a task shared by the navigator and the nose gunner. In any mission, there was always the distinct possibility of becoming separated from the group and thus having to return home alone. I had to be prepared to do my own navigation and in some cases to do the bomb dropping honors.

The usual procedure for bombing was for all aircraft to drop on a signal from the lead plane, or deputy lead in the event that the lead plane was not functional. The lead plane carried a smoke bomb. When the nose gunner saw this drop from the lead, he would press a switch that would start the orderly release of the bombs for the entire squadron. Sometimes all bombs would be dropped in a salvo. But more often they would be dropped at timed intervals so as to devastate a long and wide strip on the ground. Timing was by means of an "intervelometer." When this device indicated that all bombs had been released, it was my job to throw a switch that would assure that the intervelometer was cleared.

If one of us needed a boost in mental or physical status (such as to combat a hangover), a big "benny" was always available. Benzedrine, that is. Another aid to the hangover was sucking on the oxygen supply in the airplane before takeoff.

An opportunity was always available for prayer with the chaplain. As I recall, only a relatively small fraction of airmen participated in this. I did not. Our pilot didn't either. His comment in his memoirs was, "I figured I was too far gone and reported directly to my plane." I guess young men feel that horrible things cannot happen to them and so do not require the intervention of a supreme being. Statistics will certainly show that prayer had little to do with survival rates unless prayer interfered with the job, in which case it could have a negative effect. It is possible that, in some cases, prayer served as an antidote to shell shock. Had our culture included those with very strong religious beliefs as in Japan or Iran, fear of death might have been small enough to encourage suicide bombers. Religion will not be discussed further.

The chaplain did, however, have another role. We were subject to regular discussions and briefings separate from those preceding a mission. The chaplain was called upon to raise our sense of morality. In particular, he emphasized the importance of Boy Scout preparedness; be sure to get a supply of (free) condoms before going on a pass. One of his favorite presentations was to the effect that, when walking down the street, and if an attractive female is spotted, you already practically had the clapp or something worse. In those days, social diseases could be pretty serious and difficult to cure because we did not then have many of our modern miracle drugs. The cure for gonorrhea (clapp) was soundings up the urethra and giving the patient an illness with a high temperature. Worse than a root canal by far! How do I know? One of our crew members went through it. I won't mention names. (It wasn't me.)

Takeoff for this first mission was at 9:30 A.M. Aircraft would fly at a medium altitude over England while completing formations consisting of bomb groups, each with their two or three or four squadrons, loosely formed with other groups. B-24 and B-17 groups were not mixed because of differences in altitudes and speeds over enemy territory. We were lower but not slower.

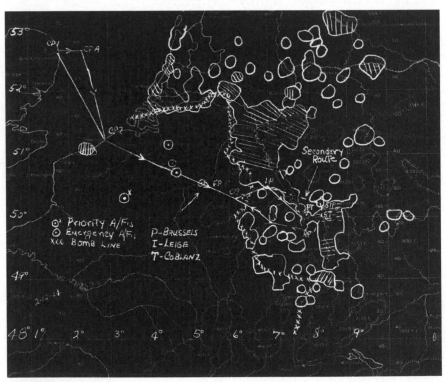

FIGURE 4-1.   Chart of mission route for Number 1, December 2, 1944.

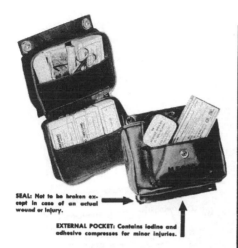

SEAL: Not to be broken except in case of an actual wound or injury.

EXTERNAL POCKET: Contains iodine and adhesive compresses for minor injuries.

CONTENTS

1. Tourniquet, (1)
2. Morphine syrette (2)
3. Wound dressing, small, (3)
4. Scissors, (1 pair)
5. Sulfanilamide crystals, envelope, (1)
6. Sulfadiazine tablets, (1 box of 12 tablets)
7. Burn ointment, (1 tube) (Boric or 5% Sulfadiazine)
8. Eye dressing set
9. Halazone tablets

1. In the case of a wound, first stop the flow of blood. The clothing should be cut away and a compress or wound dressing applied after the sulfanilamide powder has been sprinkled into the wound. If a firmly applied dressing will not cause the bleeding to stop, or if there is actual spurting of blood from an artery, the tourniquet should be applied. A tourniquet must be released every twenty minutes and removed as soon as hemorrhage stops.

2. To relieve severe pain open the small cardboard container and follow directions given there in the use of the hypodermic syrettes of morphine. Do not hesitate to use the hypodermic to relieve suffering.

3. In case of head injury have the man lie quietly with head slightly elevated.

4. In the event of marked blood loss with shock and/or unconsciousness have the man lie horizontally or lie with the head down, if possible.

5. An adequate supply of oxygen is doubly important in case of serious injury. Use it generously.

10. 1" Adhesive compresses (1 box) (Contents of small outer pocket)
11. Iodine swabs (10) (Contents of small outer pocket)

FIGURE 4-2.   First-aid kit and instructions.

Once formed, our group left the English coast, in this case at 10:45 A.M. The time required in order to get organized was typically over an hour! *Note:* We used the 24-hour system of time. I have changed this to A.M. and P.M. in order to better serve the needs of those not familiar with the 24-hour system. We also used the military convention (and civilian convention in many countries) of showing the day of the month before the month. I have also changed this. You will note that I do not use the meter-kilogram system of measurement. Nobody was concerned about this in 1944 (other than noncombat scientists and engineers). But I do routinely use nautical miles and nautical miles per hour (knots) because this is standard navigational procedure today and will probably remain so into the foreseeable future. (*Personal note:* I wish our country would convert from the size of an old English king's foot to the International System of Units! But keep the nautical measures.)

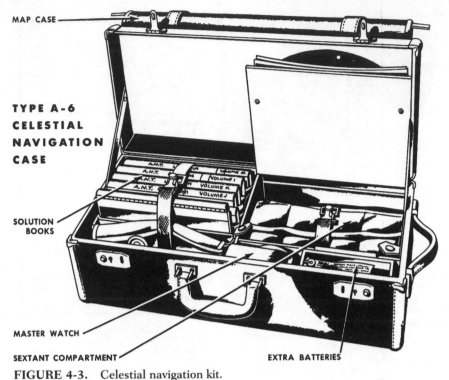

MAP CASE

TYPE A-6
CELESTIAL
NAVIGATION
CASE

SOLUTION
BOOKS

MASTER WATCH

SEXTANT COMPARTMENT

EXTRA BATTERIES

FIGURE 4-3.   Celestial navigation kit.

The flight path usually crossed the Belgian or Dutch coast with a couple of turns here and there on the way to the target. At this time we would don our flak suits and steel helmets. Preparation for bombing began from an *initial point* (IP). This point was selected so as to not reveal the particular target. From the IP we began our bomb run. During the run the planes had to be kept in tight formation without deviating if accurate bombing was to result. This would always increase the danger from antiaircraft fire. If possible, the bomb run avoided strong head winds, which often were over 100 miles per hour at the altitudes that we normally flew at. Our flight paths often encountered the jet stream. But we did not know about the jet stream back in 1944.

We bombed the target from 23,500 feet altitude and used H2X (radar) bombing because of a complete undercast with no features on the ground being visible. Only the lead plane and the deputy lead carried radar. The entire second division went to this target. We dropped a lot of chaff on the bomb run. What is *chaff*? The dictionary may not define it the way we did. It is strips of aluminum foil, a foot or so long, which return a lot of noise to gun-laying antiaircraft radar. The length of the foil strips is adjusted to best counter a particular radar frequency. Both sides of the conflict had radar during the war, especially in its later stages. The first group over a target can suffer more than followers because they have only partial protection from chaff. In some cases American-flown British Mosquito aircraft flew ahead and dropped lots of chaff, which augmented protection. In visual weather, however, chaff was only partly helpful because visual gun aiming is then possible. However, accurate range is better given by radar than visually. Chaff would at least hamper ranging.

I used G for the first 30 miles inside the Belgian coast. It was thereafter jammed. In fact, virtually all of my electronic aids were thoroughly jammed when over Germany. The rest of the mission was on dead reckoning. We saw scarecrows and Jerry (German) smoke bombs at a distance. A *scarecrow* produces a relatively large burst of black smoke with a downward spiral similar to the path of a hypothetical bomber in a terminal spin. I don't recall any report of actual damage caused by such a weapon. Perhaps their purpose was psychological.

Our bombs were away at 12:36 P.M. Wind at our altitude was 75 knots from 235 degrees. On return, we left the continental coast at 2:10 P.M. and landed at 3:15 P.M. The bomb load was twelve 500-pound, general-purpose devices. On this first mission, all of the original crew were involved except for our copilot and engineer who were replaced by more experienced instructors.

After landing, we were debriefed. What did we see that could help in future missions? What did we experience? Did we have equipment difficulties?

Then there was one final award for being alive (if we chose to receive it). This was a healthy shot of whisky or cognac, perhaps from the bootleg larder acquired by the group on returns from earlier fuel-carrying missions. This award was often sufficient to energize an excursion into town for pubbing or dancing at the Muscle Palace. The booze did provide relief from stress and no doubt reduced the danger of succumbing to a "Section 8 illness" (i.e., shell shock or similar).

The pilot and I were given a photocopy of a map showing the route and flak concentrations as previously discussed. This is all that the pilot got. I received more, namely, a more detailed map with coordinate positions. In most cases, these maps would be completed as part of the briefing. I would also keep a detailed flight log, from takeoff to final landing. This could run to 100 or more entries.

Crew members got something to help make their trip pleasant. We got a small box of hard candies, compliments of the British. These actually served a useful purpose in alleviating thirst. We did not get any water. Why not? The stuff would have frozen solid at 40 below! We could not afford the luxury of insulated and heated storage boxes. Another reason for the candy and lack of water was to avoid the need to urinate. At 40 below, such an act might end up with a frozen tool!

FIGURE 4-4. Drawing on wall of the Link Trainer room labeled with names of a "notorious" crew.

FIGURE 4-5. The character called SMOE (sad men of Europe). Don't confuse him with Kilroy. Kilroy was here and there but was never pictured.

BOMBING PHILOSOPHY

The general objective was to get all of the group's bombs within a 2000-foot radius circle about the target. Excellent bombing got all bombs for a complete bomb group within a 1000-foot circle. The degree of excellence then evaluated the percentage of the bombs that got within 500 feet. Getting all bombs within 500 feet was never accomplished for a complete bomb group. But it was, once, for a single squadron— our squadron. The bomb pattern was not always circular. We often set the intervelometer to release bombs in a timed sequence so that they would create a narrow but long path of destruction.

All things being equal, bombing accuracy decreases with altitude. The Liberator achieved generally superior accuracy to the Flying Fortress for the simple reason that we usually flew at considerably lower altitudes.

The H2X radar was not very accurate in bombing, rarely within the 2000-foot circle. If we were after a marshalling yard in the middle of a town and could not see the surface, the bombing would attempt to straddle the rail lines by extending the path over a distance of a mile or so. If our group flew 27 aircraft with 12 bombs each, the result was 324 bombs of 500 pounds each, at least a few of which might damage the rail yard. Then add other groups in our wing to the carnage.

What would happen to a city or town unfortunate enough to have a marshalling yard? We should have known that we must be killing many women, children, and elderly. Looking back now, I find it difficult to recall how we managed to erase such thoughts from our minds. Everything was kill. We never talked about the side effects of our actions. In fact, we tended to revel in them. The present-day "do-gooders" will be horrified. They were not there, and they were not being frightened by the possibility of being killed themselves. All I can say about latter-day objectors is that they are naive. Had we known what the Germans were doing to Jews and other ethnic groups, we might have been even more eager to destroy anything and everything German. The pain brought forth by this knowledge of German inhumanity had to wait until final victory. (Hollywood movies tend to fictionalize our concern for women and children. We really didn't think about trying to avoid schools and hospitals.)

In all fairness and in spite of propaganda to the contrary, I don't think we were any better or any worse than the Germans or the Japanese in our bombing philosophy. We all killed the innocent without remorse (at the time).

AREA BOMBING

The British air force bombed mostly at night. Although the original intent was to do strategic bombing, aiming accuracy was so poor that desired targets were rarely hit. The problem was trying to see targets in a blacked-out area, especially when clouds partly or completely obstructed the view. Radar was not adequate to the task. In effect, bombing was on an area basis without much control over the kinds of targets that were hit (homes, hospitals, schools, etc.).

The Germans staged a major raid on Coventry, England, in November, 1940. This was a very viable strategic target because so much heavy industry was (is) located there. The raid was widely described in America as being horrible. Such stories were clearly propaganda meant to raise our sense of sympathy for the English. (No one at the time mentioned the heavy industry that was damaged.)

An analysis by the British showed that productivity was more affected by loss of homes than by destruction of factories! It was calculated that, for each ton of bombs, 100 to 200 people were made homeless. One analysis concluded that morale suffered more from loss of a home than loss of friends or even relatives!

This calculation changed the English bombing strategy from precision strategic bombing (which they failed at in any event) to area bombing without any serious attempt to avoid residential areas. This change in strategy was championed by Air Chief Marshal Arthur Harris with direct and enthusiastic support from Winston Churchill. When possible, a meaningful strategic target was specified as an aiming point, but it was realized that it might be missed, in which case bombs would destroy homes and lower morale.

Although our 8th air force daylight bombing missions could accurately pinpoint targets in clear weather, accuracy became poor in the presence of an undercast. Our radar wasn't all that good. Even though unintentional, the result was that we too did area bombing. Perhaps our own leaders secretly subscribed to the tactics of "Bomber" Harris. I can repeat an earlier statement to the effect that our bombing philosophy was neither better nor worse than that of our enemies.

ANNOUNCEMENT

The military does get around to letting the folks back home know where their sons or daughters have gone. The announcement in my case appeared in the *Pasadena Star News* on February 15, 1945. It reads:

> Second Lieutenant John L. Stewart, son of Mr. and Mrs. John P. Stewart, 1005 South Oak Knoll Avenue, is serving as navigator of a B-24 Liberator bomber of the 467th Bomb Group

commanded by Col. Albert J. Shower, a unit of the 2nd
Bombardment Division of the 8th Air Force in England.
Lieutenant Stewart entered service in June, 1943, and won
his wings at Hondo, Tex., Army Air Field last July. He had his
crew training at Pueblo, Colo., and went overseas last
October. Lieutenant Stewart was born in Pasadena and
attended McKinley Elementary and Junior High and Pasadena
Junior College. He enlisted in the Air Force while he was in
his first year at college. The division of which he is now a
member is commanded by Maj. Gen. William E. Kepner and
his group has flown on 180 combat missions over Germany
and enemy territory in the past eight months.

A POEM

The following poem was written by a member of a small writers' group that included my mother and my aunt. In the poem,
I am Larry and Rendy is my first cousin. I don't know the
other names.

HERITAGE

BY DOROTHY MARIE DAVIS

The world was nothing till they gave it to me—
These sons and nephews—in extravagance.
For Larry, England's skies sag, bleak and gloomy,
And where Herb waded I discovered France.
Now Italy's a landing field for Bill;
Russia is safety where hurt planes can light.
The Breadth and wealth and challenge of Brazil
Are Raymond, only. Oh, I know it's quite
Disgraceful to admit such tunnel vision.
One should see great significances where
Poor mankind staggers in a world collision;
I only see Joe's dark, wind-tumbled hair.
And Burma is a place where Chuck has grown
To manhood, by his notes. Luzon's the land
Where Jim marched cruelly, waited all alone.
And Rendy's boots climbed Iwo's ashen sand.
My world was bounded by familiar fences—

Our Street, Our Town, Our School, and,
half-recalled,
The scenes of childhood. Those were my defenses,
But now the world is wider and unwalled.
Bill's there . . . and Larry . . . and a flag's
unfurled;
Fences are lost, but I have found the world.

THE NEXT FEW

Missions are grouped in clusters of six. For every six, you are awarded a medal for still being alive. The Air Medal is for the first six, and you get an oak leaf cluster on the ribbon for each additional six. At the end of the war, I had only three ribbons, European Theater with three battle stars, Air Medal with four oak leaf clusters, and an American Theater ribbon. I am not sure why I warranted the last one. Perhaps it was because I was in the Air Transport Command for a couple of weeks after returning home. I am amused by the chestfulls seen on modern-day officers. The criteria for earning these are somewhat obscure to me. Maybe the purpose of all these medals is to indicate length of service, like hash marks on the sleeves of enlisted personnel.

MISSION NUMBER 2: DECEMBER 4, 1944, BEBRA, GERMANY

The target was another marshalling yard at Bebra, Germany. The load was 10, 500-pound general-purpose bombs (GPs) and 2, 500-pound incendiary clusters. We had a maximum effort with 36 planes in the air. Our group led the division. Takeoff was at 9:05 A.M. We had trouble with our number 2 engine and barely got off the runway. Engine problems plagued us on and off throughout the mission, which was not conducive to a sense of security. We nearly lost the engine several times, even on the bomb run. Our climb to assembly was slow due to the engine problem. We finally left the English coast at 10:45 A.M. and reached the continent at 11:30 A.M. Penetration

FIGURE 5-1. Navigator's wings and ribbons: Air Medal with four oak leaf clusters, American Theater ribbon, and European Theater ribbon with three battle stars.

was deep. There were no flak or fighters, although these were expected. The P-51 fighter cover was beautiful, which greatly pleased our pilot who preferred this model fighter over the P-47. My G box burned out early in the flight. *Data:* H2X bombing from 23,000 feet. Temperature was −35 degrees centigrade. Wind was 90 knots from 300 degrees. Bombs away at 12:43 P.M. and return to base at 4:00 P.M. Of the 2700 gallons of fuel we had at the start, only 200 remained at the end. This was the first mission for our copilot. Our regular nose gunner, Sgt. Philmore Zilbert, was replaced on this mission.

It is noted that we did take chances. The critical nature of our many missions called for less caution than would be tolerated in other situations. Normal prudence would not have permitted continuing the flight with a sick engine.

Note on temperature: We always used the centigrade scale where zero is the freezing point of water versus 32 degrees for the Fahrenheit scale. Most of the time we were quite cold at altitude. Conversion between scales is not difficult at 40 below. The same number, 40 below, applies to both scales.

MISSION NUMBER 3: DECEMBER 6, 1944, BIELEFELD, GERMANY

This was somewhat unusual because only our original radio operator, Cpl. Buckman, and I were from our own crew. The rest were from many other crews, some of whom were getting in their final mission. The pilot, Lt. Gannett, was on his last mission. He was good. The ship was clean and in good shape

FIGURE 5-2. The author in mild weather flying togs with parachute harness. Pueblo, Colorado, before going overseas.

FIGURE 5-3.   Bomb bursts on Hamburg. An example of precision bombing.

as well. Maybe I should have been concerned. Stories are often told of the crew member who gets killed on his last mission!

The target was another railway marshalling yard in Bielefeld, Germany. We had only two squadrons on this effort, 18 aircraft total. Our squadron led the group that led the division that led the wing. Our bomb load was eight 1000-pound GPs. *Other data:* Temperature −34 degrees centigrade and wind of 50 knots from 290 degrees. The load was our maximum normal bomb-carrying capacity, namely, eight 1000-pound bombs. An equivalent in weight but much more devastating per explosion was a load of four 2000-pounders. When we carried 250- or 500-pound bombs, the total load was less than 8000 pounds because of the limited size of the bomb bays.

We left the English coast at 10:45 A.M. Flak near the Dutch coast was meager but very accurate. Two planes received flak damage, and one lost its hydraulic system. Our primary target was a viaduct 500 feet long and 70 feet high carrying 3 tracks. It was located about 4 miles northeast of the town. It was our first priority, but it had to be visual in order to bomb it. This viaduct was carrying the bulk of the traffic from Hamburg and cities in northern Germany to the front. Holland going in and coming out was mostly visual but then it became 10/10 undercast (100 percent) until we got almost to the target. Because of clouds, we dropped on the secondary target, the marshalling yard adjacent to the town, using an alternative form of blind bombing called *PFF* (and I confess to not knowing how this works). Halfway on the bomb run, the weather cleared, and we saw the bombs hit the yard. The target was extensively damaged along with a good part of the town. Our squadron's bombs hit slightly to the left of the target, which contributed to the massive destruction of the town itself. Other groups were more successful. The target, which was extensively damaged, carried the same traffic as crossed the viaduct, but the damage was not as permanent. This is another instance where we probably killed a lot of innocent civilians. But we managed to keep thoughts of this kind out of our minds and might even have been guilty of hiding a form of black pleasure.

We were in the air for 6 hours and wore flak suits almost the entire time we were over the continent. We lost our interphone, but we were able to switch to the command line. No German fighters. Excellent P-51 and P-47 fighter cover. I gave approximate locations of V2 sites in debriefing.

MISSION NUMBER 4: DECEMBER 12, 1944, HANAU, GERMANY

This target had been hit before and was to be hit again in order to destroy railway repair equipment and specialized personnel. We carried 12, 500-pound GPs. The bombing was visual, and the pattern of explosions was near perfect. The trip was uneventful, and there were only a few bursts of inaccurate flak.

The bad part was that I could hardly navigate. No G box. No calibration cards. No astrocompass mount. And, of course, no seat (which was typical). The lead navigator did a lot of wandering about, which made following quite difficult. Except for the target area, most of the trip was under 10/10 conditions.

MISSION NUMBER 5: DECEMBER 24, 1944, GEROLSTEIN, GERMANY

Christmas Eve. Special greetings were written in chalk on each of our 24, 250-pound GPs. Since the recent German counterattacks on the Western Front (i.e., the start of the Battle of the Bulge), our troops were hard-pressed and in a bad situation. To make matters worse, weather had been so bad that we (and the 8th Air Force) had flown only one mission in the previous 12 days. But on this day, weather was perfect: clear and visibility unlimited (CAVU). Every group in the entire 8th Air Force hit a different, rather small but important, target. The first and third divisions (B-17s) hit airfields, and the second (B-24s) hit railways and small marshalling yards. These yards were close to our front lines and of immense importance. We pasted our target. (*Short note:* Since the end of the war, I have heard of another definition for CAVU: "severe clear.")

We managed to get almost every plane in our group into the air. This included "War Wearies" and even our assembly ship "Big Pete," which had no guns. ("Little Pete" was a P-47 used in assembling squadrons prior to departure from England.) In order to provide a sense of security for the crew in Big Pete, the waist gunners were each given one (only) carbine. Our group was able to create seven squadrons separated into two groups for two different targets: about 60 aircraft. Only one ship had to abort the mission, which attests to excellent aircraft maintenance.

We saw no flak, but five holes were found in the ship on our wing, and the lead ship lost its radar ball. Flak killed one crew member in the group, and earned purple hearts for a couple of other crew members. Fighters hit a group 15 minutes ahead of us. By chance of fate, we were 15 minutes late

FIGURE 5-4.   Christmas Eve, 1944. Every flyable plane sent out to bomb.

over the target. More aircraft were over Germany this day, heavies, mediums, and fighters, then ever before. We flew "L'il Peach," a very war-weary craft.

Christmas Day. We did not fly this one. Fighters hit our group, and we lost 3 out of 18 with only one of the three crews surviving. I felt guilty about not being on this mission because we were having a pleasant dinner with an English family (described later).

December 29, 1944. I will come back to this bloody "non-mission" after describing Number 6.

MISSION NUMBER 6: DECEMBER 30, 1944, NEUWIED, GERMANY

The target was a railroad bridge over a small river where it emptied into the Rhine, about 8 miles northwest of Koblenz.

This is a major city in the northern part of the Rhur Valley. This region was (and is) Germany's principal area for heavy manufacturing. Understandably, it had more than its share of antiaircraft weapons. Weather was 5/10 to the continent and 10/10 everywhere else. We bombed by G2X with six 1000-pound bombs. Surprisingly, this mission was uneventful, without flak or fighters. It was the easiest one so far. Flight time was only 5½ hours. The only dangerous part was our landing, somewhat off the runway and skidding back on. Being my sixth, I earned the Air Medal.

One of our buddies, a crew that came to England with us, did not make it back. They lost an engine and were last reported to be icing up heavily at 1500 feet. They were attempting to reach Brussels.

FIGURE 5-5. Witchcraft. Over 200 missions without an abort.

BLOODY NONMISSION AND PILOT'S LAMENT: DECEMBER 29, 1944

We got up and briefed for a very important target at the base of Runsted's salient (near the town of Prum, Germany). No one doubted the necessity of bombing his supply lines. All that remained between him and the North Sea were cooks and bakers. One of our squadrons took off, and then it settled. Fog. Fog so thick you could not see the edge of the road or the edge of a taxiway or runway. We were told to start engines and taxi for group departure. The fog was so thick that we taxied into a *hardstand* by mistake (which is a concrete parking place with direct taxiway access). This was the first incident that worked to possibly spare our lives.

I did not enter this story in my small black diary. But I did write it down on the back of the mission chart. However, rather than giving my account, I defer to the pilot as he remembered it. John Belingheri was the one trying to taxi and worrying about takeoff. Some incidents are not told quite correctly because his memoirs were written 45 or more years after the incident.

> There was one mission I'll never forget. I don't remember the date or what the target was. Everything was the same as a normal mission that morning except it was foggy and no breeze. The visibility was less than 10 feet and the window glasses on the plane were all fogged over. It was almost impossible to see the ground from the cockpit. We were all sure the mission would be scrubbed and were extremely surprised when we saw the start engine flare. My crew was #4 for takeoff that morning and we taxied out in proper position. But because of the frost on the windshield I was unable to see the plane in front of me and I was afraid of hitting it. So I turned it over to my copilot to taxi while I cleaned the windshield so I could see. The copilot had the same trouble and in order to keep going he opened his side window and was taxiing by looking down at the edge of the taxi way. What he forgot was that the edge would lead him into a hardstand (parking place for planes). This caused us to lose two spots in our takeoff position, and now, instead of #4, we

FIGURE 5-6.   Hardstand at Rackheath.

were #6. There was no vision, and we were heavily loaded and
with less than 5000 feet to takeoff. It would be close. At the
end of the runway was a large bunch of trees. As #1 took off, he
couldn't get off the ground because of the conditions of load
and wind. He ended up in the trees in a burning mess. Before
the tower knew what was going on (no visibility), #2 and 3 and
4 lined up to go and went. Besides everything else, we now had
a propwash condition on the runway from the plane in front of
us. (Propwash is the air stirred up by a propeller and just
knocks you all over.) About this time, the tower got wise that
something was wrong at the end of the runway, and they
stopped the takeoffs and we were told to shut our engines
down. We were #1 for takeoff at this time. All the planes that
tried to take off in front of us were in the trees at the end of the
runway stacked up on each other and burning. Ninety percent
of the crews were blown apart. We would have been the fourth
to blow up if it had not been for my copilot's error.

While we were waiting to see what happened, my tail gunner took the gas can for the put-put and dumped it. He also removed the gas from the put-put itself. Suddenly, we were told to start our engines and continue takeoff. We couldn't because of no put-put. With a lot of loud words, the takeoff officer sent for a gallon of gas, but before he got back, the base commander saw what was happening and scrubbed the mission. We got our gas, started up, and taxied back to our hardstand position.

The squadron C.O. came by and told me to find out who pulled the gas deal on our plane and raise hell with him. We told him who did it, but it was told at the nearest pub. He got drunk as hell, and he didn't have to buy a drink. That was that! We cheated the odds twice that day by two "stupid" mistakes. Ho, Ho, Ho, like a fox, the tail gunner.

A couple of details are not remembered quite correctly by the pilot. My log says that the first six or seven planes got off OK before the four doomed ones. Of these four, two crashed and exploded with the crew members killed. One got off but crash landed later with some injuries. The fourth one managed to get airborn, but the crew bailed out with the plane abandoned to crash somewhere. The pilot is correct, however, in that we were first in line for takeoff after shutting down our engines, with several aircraft waiting behind us.

What is a *put-put*? It is an auxiliary two-cylinder gasoline engine used to maintain battery charge and to supply electric power when main engines are not operating.

I am not certain that the person who is said to have drained the put-put was the tail gunner. If I had guessed who it might have been, I would have chosen the engineer who was the person normally responsible for put-put maintenance. John, the pilot, does not state my suspicion, but I think that it was he who gave the order to kill the put put! If so, then he is the real hero in my eyes. Lord knows how many lives were saved, ours and those in planes behind us, by the "brilliant" act of someone in our crew. And that opportunity would not have come had we not taxied into a hardstand by mistake. We would probably have been one of the earlier basket cases.

Later that day, one could see (and smell) rows of blackened bodies collected on a grassy knoll. Time for booze.

A COMMENT

Just how hazardous is a blind takeoff? Here is how you might try to do it. Line up the plane with the runway. Set your gyro-compass. Then proceed at full throttle while keeping heading at the original gyro setting. When you have enough speed, rotate and hope you clear whatever is at the end or near the edges of the runway. The initial problem, and in fact the major problem, is trying to line up with the runway. How do you do this if you can't see the edge? You might try to line up with a white line painted on the runway, but you can see only a few feet of this. Our runways were not very wide. Length was limited to about 4500 feet. What happens if you are only 1 degree out of alignment? You can follow the gyro to 1 degree so this is not the major problem. One degree error after 4000 feet figures to be 70 feet. Starting at the center of the runway, this is enough to put you over the edge and headed for oblivion. Thank you blundering copilot and the put-put drainer whoever you are!

Ours was not the only group to suffer tragedy resulting from attempting to take off in fog. I have recently read an account by a crew member of the 453rd Bomb Group. It was January 13, 1945. They were number 3 for takeoff. They managed it. But the next two aircraft crashed on takeoff, and the base was closed. The account stated that visibility was not more than 150 feet and sometimes less. Our situation on December 29 had a visibility much less than this!

ANOTHER COMMENT

The number of airmen in our group killed at the end of the runway on December 29 was one of the largest in a single day ever recorded for the 467th Bomb Group. Nowhere in the records as far as I have been able to determine is the cause of this disaster mentioned. No reason of a combat nature, or any other reason for that matter, is expressed in Allan Healy's book (see Chapter Six). In fact, no comments of any kind relate to deaths on December 29. Such errors are rarely advertised, whether related to the air force or the army or any other military group. Nor are such mistakes ever admitted when some civilian agency such as the police or CIA commits a blunder. But we know what happened. The record is no longer sealed.

INTERLUDE

ORIGINS OF THE GROUP

This is a good place to stop and talk about other things besides the blow-by-blow account of the fight. Here and in other parts of this book, I am indebted to an officer by the name of Capt. Allan Healy, who was a security officer, not an air crew member. He organized and then privately published a book recounting the history of the 467th from its inception until it was finally disbanded after the war. I will try to give credits in cases where I use material directly or in support of my own perceptions. I am also borrowing some of the photographs, a few of which duplicate my own and which, I believe, originated as official air force photographs and hence "belong" only to the U.S. government.

The 467th was formed at an open prairie base near Mountain Home, Idaho, in September, 1943. Key flying personnel trained in Orlando, Florida. When elements from Idaho and Florida were combined, the group began to look like one. Molding the group into a fighting force was done at Wendover, Utah, near the Nevada border, an unbelievably godforsaken place. In February, 1944, the nonflyers got their marching orders and traveled by boat, a C-3 freighter, leaving February 28. It took 8 days and lots of seasickness to get to England. The assignment was Rackheath.

The men with the airplanes enjoyed a transatlantic flight via Trinidad. From Trinidad they crossed the Amazon river to Belem, Brazil, where they were restricted to the base. From there, they crossed the Atlantic to Dakar, Senegambia, where they were again restricted to the base. Two aircraft had mechanical problems but eventually were able to rejoin the group. After Dakar, the next stop was Marrakech, Morocco. On the way, one plane flew into the Atlas mountains and all aboard were killed. Another had an accident on takeoff with four killed. From Marrakech the flight went via Scotland to Wales with guns at the ready as they flew around Portugal and Spain. The final flight was from Wales to Rackheath.

We don't learn much in school about the Atlas mountains. Perhaps a little geography is worthwhile. The *Encyclopedia Britannica* has four pages of fine print and a map on these mountains and their peoples, the ancestral home of the Berbers. The range stretches from the Atlantic Ocean in Morocco to the Mediterranean in the border region between Algeria and Tunisia. Some 1200 miles long, peaks soar to almost 14,000 feet in Morocco, dropping to a more consistent level in the 6000-foot range into Algeria. The northwest side has rain and snow, even down to 6500 feet for part of the year. The opposite side of the range is rocky and arid. There is not much vegetation or wildlife, partly because of thousands of years of human occupation. Generally the population is "dirt" poor, and the region can properly be called "overpopulated." A constant stream of "surplus people" seeks employment in the northern lowlands and cities.

In mythology, Atlas was condemned to hold up the sky for participating in a war with Zeus. Atlas was presumably king of his mountains. Finally, Atlas was turned to a rocky mountain by Perseus. Confusing but still interesting!

East Anglia is everything you have heard about the English countryside, full of farms with woods and hedgerows. Pheasants were about, along with rabbits that come out in the late evenings. Norwich is at the heart of Norfolk County. It is both an ancient and a modern city. Norfolk County is beautifully treed with winding rivers and lakes. Our wing, the 96th of the Second Division of the 8th Air Force, with its three bomb groups, had bases surrounding Norwich with Division Headquarters at Ketteringham Hall west of Norwich. (*Note*

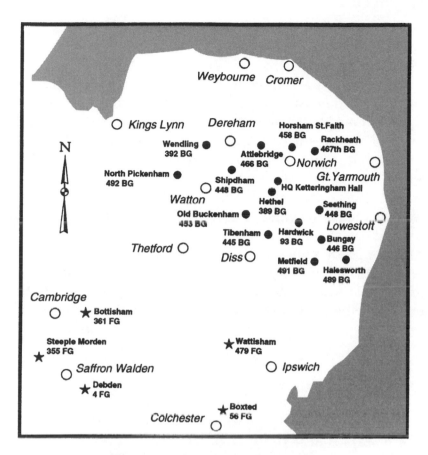

2nd Air Division Bases

44th Shipdham	453rd Old Buckenham
93rd Hardwick	458th Horsham St.Faith
389th Hethel	466th Attlebridge
392nd Wendling	467th Rackheath
445th Tibenham	489th Halesworth
446th Bungay	491st Metfield
448th Seething	492nd North Pickenham

HQ. Ketteringham Hall

Fighter Groups 65th Fighter Wing

4th Debden	355th Steeple Morden
56th Boxted	361st Bottisham

479th Wattisham

FIGURE 6-1.   Map of East Anglia showing air bases.

again: I don't know where the big numbers such as 96 wings come from.) The 466th was at Attlebridge, the 458th at Horsham St. Faith, and the 467th (ours) at Rackheath. Ours was one of the nearest bases to hostile shores. We often flew over the English coastal city of Great Yarmouth going to and coming from our jobs. The folks at this place were a bit trigger happy and would on occasion send some shells skyward toward us. We would sometimes "get even" by dropping bags of certain substances on them, generated after seven or eight hours of flying. I don't recall that anything serious happened to us from their projectiles. I don't know if what we dropped had any lasting stench.

The group's first mission was in April, 1944. The target was an aircraft assembly plant in Central France. It was a milk run. When D-Day finally came on the 6th of June, 1944, the 467th was a seasoned organization with a record of excellent bombing accuracy. But there were costs with a number of bombers and their crews lost.

The Germans contained the invasion until July 18 when the British attacked in force. The American breakout was on July 25. The whole air force went after German tactical targets. Using fragmentation bombs along with the deafening sounds of explosions, the 467th scattered and demoralized Germans and helped pave the way for General Bradley's men. Bombing continued through August. September 11 marked the 112th mission by the 467th, all in little more than 140 days at a cost of 27 aircraft. Even at this level, these losses were the smallest of any group in the 8th Air Force. And the 467th was constantly getting commendations for bombing accuracy.

The group went off combat on September 11 and began trucking gasoline to the rapidly advancing forces in France. You can imagine the unbounded joy experienced by the air crew members over cognac, perfume, German trophies, and, most important, pretty French ladies. It was rumored that a bar of soap could get almost anything. But the joy was short-lived. On October 3, the group started on its road to finish the second 100 missions.

STRESS AND STRAIN

There is no question that the life of a combat air crew member was stressful. We knew that the chances of survival over the course of 30 or 35 missions were considerably less than 100 percent. How we dealt with this depended on individual psychological factors. There really was no common or standard attitude.

One palliative was a form of denial; thoughts of getting killed were purged from the mind. Each of us younger flyers had the advantage of believing that we were immune to harm, not unlike young people today who seek thrills through dangerous pursuits.

When on an actual mission, I was in a way more fortunate than other crew members. I was far too busy to think about dying, even in the presence of flak and fighters. I did not try to get into the minds of other crew members who had little to do except watch and ponder the approaching threats. And besides, I was young, naive, and certainly not skilled in the psychologist's trade.

FIGURE 6-2.   Approach to Tower Bridge in London.

When not on an actual or practice mission, latent fears could be subordinated by keeping mentally very busy (or asleep). For many of us this was achieved by comradeship at the club or various pubs. Booze was the principal catharsis. Chasing was another pursuit with motivations that took over the mind like a lion stalking its prey. Of course, these activities are common in the peacetime military as well as at college fraternities.

Another way that we were kept from thinking too much about the hazards of our jobs was through meetings of the ground school kind and practice missions, especially the practice missions. With little doubt, "practice makes perfect," and this practice contributed to our outstanding record for bombing accuracy. Whether or not higher-ups prescribed practice as a palliative to stress remains unknown to me.

Our regular group parties also helped to keep us from thinking by, in part, getting us to place our minds in an anticipation mode. At these parties we could combine comradeship, booze, and chasing. Our group was perhaps the premier practitioner of this form of diversion, with our reputation being broadcast far and wide.

Some crew members assumed a more passive and withdrawn pattern of behavior, some combining this with religion. Without the safety valves that us boozers and chasers utilized, the quiet ones must have suffered considerably greater anguish. Were these individuals more likely to suffer emotional problems during their military days and perhaps long after? I really don't know. All of us carried some kind of mind wounds for years after the end of the war. The severity of these was a matter of degree, from almost nothing to total debilitation.

Some of the emotional problems carried to civilian life by veterans may have little to do with combat experience. Taking a young man from a quiet and staid and dependent family life, shoving him into the world, giving him a sense of power and importance, and then dumping him back from whence he came, is of itself an emotionally jarring experience. Perhaps a fair faction of lingering problems displayed by some veterans trace to this experience and not to combat, if any.

Somewhere near the middle of one's tour, operational fatigue came to most of us. This was the result of a combination of factors, the exhausting effect of the tension, frequent briefings, flying at low altitude, loss of sleep, and practice and real missions. This was probably about half and half caused by simple fatigue and the emotional strain. No shame was associated with being a little "flak-happy." The air force invented the "flak shack," a most appealing country estate where leisure, good food, and pleasant surroundings helped to get one's head back on straight. Alternatives were a trip to London or some other area in England where pubs and girls abounded. None of our crew members went to a flak shack. Instead we went to London and little town pubs in and around Norwich. We all had bicycles or used local buses for the necessary travel to these little, out-of-the-way drinking establishments. The calming and curing effects were comparable. Members of the "Land Army" were every bit as supportive as any young lady in London.

And what was the Land Army? With so many country boys drafted and sent to far corners of the earth, farm labor became scarce. The limited land suitable for agriculture in England had to be treasured and nurtured for maximum possible productivity. Older folks and younger females were pressed into service. We, of course, preferred the young ladies. But we liked everyone in the pubs.

RACKHEATH AND SURROUNDING AREAS

Our base was on lands owned by Sir Edward Stacey. He lived in an imposing mansion surrounded by truly beautiful grounds, especially the pond. We enjoyed somewhat less luxurious accommodations in Nissen (Quanset) huts. I took a few pictures of huts and buddies, in one case with female visitors.

The winter of 1944–1945 was an especially severe one. It is not too easy to build a large snowman in England because England does not get that much snow at any one time. I took a picture of a large snowman outside of our hut. Enough said.

We had one small coke stove in the center of each hut and a ration of two buckets of fuel per week. A hut held officers from

FIGURE 6-3. Copilot Lt. Vernon Mason.

three air crews. Enlisted men were housed separately in barracks. We had an officer's club, and enlisted men had theirs.
We weren't always out on the town. The club offered friendly
interchange with liquids that helped one to relax. Considerable
time was spent in our huts, often crowded about the little stove.
We had radios and could listen to the American Forces radio or
the German station in Luxembourg whose primary mission was
to discourage us and lower our morale. Actually, I think it did
just the opposite, especially when it would abruptly cease to
transmit when the RAF planes flew over on their way to important targets in Germany. We did the daylight stuff. The RAF
continued at night—a sort of double whammy!

FIGURE 6-4. A large snowman next to hut.

FIGURE 6-5. Another crew in our hut.

We also had a respectable movie theater. The high point was the monthly dances that we held complete with our own orchestra, the "Airliners." Base trucks ferried girls from Norwich and surrounding areas and took them home (at least most of them). And we had occasional USO shows. Dance halls near the base and in Norwich were wonderful. A liberty run of trucks made getting to and from Norwich easy, but we were just as likely to take the local English bus.

Norwich was only a short bus ride away. The premier destination was the Sampson and Hercules dance hall. We referred to it as "Muscle Palace." This well-run dance hall was like similar places in our own country before the big band era ended and before a growing number of trouble-makers all but ruined these places of social interaction where one could meet young ladies with some hope for developing lasting relationships. Some of our people did in fact find true love in England with subsequent marriage. The officers of our own crew were a different breed, still acting like immature kids at a socially oriented college fraternity. Indeed, we had dates with activities of various kinds, but not usually with long-range motives in mind.

FIGURE 6-6.   Author entertaining guests in the hut.

FIGURE 6-7.   Rackheath party. Col. Shower and friend dancing.

FIGURE 6-8.   Bombardier front. Author and Carol behind.

FIGURE 6-9.   More party. Copilot on right.

FIGURE 6-10.   More party. Bombardier on right.

Whether as a primary objective or as part of a dance hall evening, we visited the pubs. If one goes to England, even today, visiting pubs provides a singular view into the English and their customs. Before TV, the church and/or the pub served as primary social gathering places. Since the church is not always open, especially in the evening, the pub became the center of society. No matter how small the hamlet, it will have a pub. A city or town will have one each couple of blocks. Unfortunately, pubs no longer serve the same purposes as they once did. The advent of TV changed that because people tended to stay at home—TV became an "antisocial" instrument.

A night (or day) on the town held more than simply beer and dancing. There was always fish and chips, wrapped in a newspaper. The British also put on many stage shows, reminiscent of Vaudeville. I recall at one of these that I was "conned" into going on stage where I acted generally foolish. The booze did it!

There was more to see in Norwich. It is a very old town with many items of historic interest. It has a beautiful cathedral and a walled inner city. Its streets are narrow. The marketplace was like that now seen in developing nations, and a bit like the "Saturday Market" in our own country. I must admit that I (and my crew) didn't do too much sightseeing of historical and special places. Our quest led in different directions. I don't suppose that history interests too many young men, not then and perhaps even less so today. Getting older changes one's outlook!

The thing that each of us had was a bicycle. These were not for getting to Norwich. Rather, they served to get us to the many pubs in the small hamlets that dotted the countryside. An idea of the importance of these to us is given with a picture of a bike roundup after most of us had left to go home after the fighting stopped. Clearly, we could not take these with us. In order to avoid unemployment in postwar England, all of these bikes were bulldozed into scrap.

Country pubs were the most fun. There usually were some land army girls with whom we could socialize and

FIGURE 6-11.   T/Sgt. Leighty and "Bing." Owners Maude and Charlie in window of "Horseshoes Inn."

FIGURE 6-12.   Maude, Charlie, and various characters.

FIGURE 6-13.   Bunch that haunted the inn. *Left to right:* Sgt. Leighty, "Bing," Sgt. Page, Lt. "Woodrow," author, and Sgt. Chastain.

FIGURE 6-14. Other customers at Horseshoes Inn.

FIGURE 6-15. The quintessential older pub customer.

FIGURE 6-16.   Street scene in older part of Norwich.

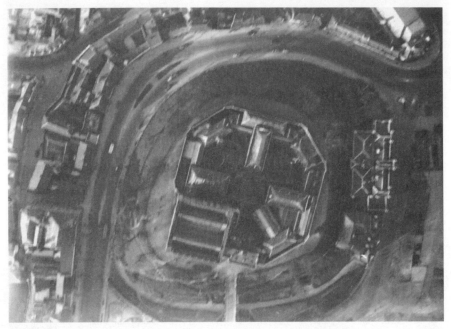

FIGURE 6-17.   Air view of castle in Norwich.

befriend. Unfortunately, we could not do much biking with snow all about. This phase of our time in England had to wait until spring, or at least until a stretch of decent weather occurred. The time span covering bike pubbing for me was not too long, ending prior to June 10, 1945, when I left by B-24 for home.

And what was London like? This took a 2-day pass, minimum. We all saw the principal sights: Tower of London, London Bridge (now in Arizona), Tower Bridge, the Thames, and lots of destruction. And, of course, Piccadilly. The problem with this place was that it sprang to life at night. The blackouts made getting about quite difficult, along with negotiating. Night in London was therefore confined to lighted places such as pubs, "bottle clubs," and dance halls. And there were plenty of these. Restaurants? We had to eat. But the fare was not what you would call three star! And eating out could be expensive—all à la carte.

WERE WE LIKED?

Did we meet local families and converse with them? Certainly.
Not in London but in Norwich and little towns. The family
members were likely to have a son or two somewhere in Africa
or France or Germany, and some grieved. They could not have

FIGURE 6-18.   Another street scene in Norwich.

FIGURE 6-19. Norwich marketplace.

been more hospitable, sharing their meager rations with us. Sometimes we would bring them something as well. Cigarettes were always welcomed. We got four or five packs a week. I was then a fairly heavy smoker but quit for good in the early 1960s. Had I not quit, I don't think I would be writing this now because one has difficulty with a pad and pencil when confined to a coffin.

The children seemed to love us. They would suddenly appear with the request for "gum chum?" A few people wished we would go away. This minority was likely to consist of English military personnel who made considerably less money than we did and who found it difficult to compete for feminine attention. The British saying about us was "Overpaid, oversexed, and over here." I suppose that, if the tables were turned, I would be resentful as well.

But the English in general were most appreciative. They realized full well that, had it not been for our assistance, starting with the "Lend Lease" program, they would probably have succumbed to German aggression. A poem by A. P. Herbert (famed English author and Member of Parliament) was widely

FIGURE 6-20.   Norwich cathedral.

FIGURE 6-21.   Bike roundup at time base was deactivated.

circulated after the war. It describes their feelings quite well and is worthy of reproduction:

Good-bye, GI—Good-bye, big-hearted Joe.
We're glad you came. We hope you're sad to go.
Say what you can for this old-fashioned isle;
And when you can't—well, say it with a smile.
Good-bye, GI—and now you know the way,
Come back and see us in a brighter day,
When England's free, and Scotch is cheap but strong,
And you can bring your pretty wives along.
Good-bye, GI, don't leave us quite alone,
Somewhere in England we must write a stone,
"Here Britain was Invaded by the Yanks,"
And under that a big and brilliant 'Thanks.'

CAROL

Let me backtrack to Christmas Day. We didn't fly this one, which turned out to be rough, losing over 10 percent of the 27 aircraft that flew this mission. The copilot and I were dining with an English family and did not hear the bad news until it was over.

From time to time, air crew members were invited to homes in the area to share food and talk. The practice was enhanced on a day like Christmas. The copilot and I signed up and were invited to the Vicar's home in a nearby hamlet, available by local bus. We knew that rations were in short supply so we took with us what we could: candy, cigarettes, and two cans of fruit (obtained by devious means).

The dinner table held us, the Vicar, his wife, two early teen children, and a niece by the name of Carol. She had recently been widowed, thanks to a shell fragment in Italy. Her home was in Cornwall, but her late husband had been stationed in the Rackheath area. I feature her in particular because this dinner resulted in later dates and trips as a kind of vacation romance.

The combination of being on active duty with a schedule that could change day by day, plus the miserable cold and snow, limited the things we could do. But we could socialize at pubs, theaters, and dances, including those that we held at Rackheath.

The notes that I kept did not include most noncombat activities, and so some details of our relationship may not be correct. I must also admit that the interlude with Carol was never mentioned to my wife. Most of us guys don't talk about romantic episodes predating marriage. But we are now old enough to reveal such escapades without fear of recrimination.

When the weather improved in early spring, it was possible to enjoy the countryside, walking or riding on bicycles. In late spring we could try canoeing on local lakes and rivers. (I wasn't much good at canoeing.)

After we flew the last mission of the war, April 25, 1945, Carol and I made a trip to her home area of Cornwall. This was not meant as an approval of me by her relatives. We both knew this was an interlude helping her to overcome grief and helping me to keep my head on straight. Travel guides point out that the best time to visit Cornwall is from early May through summer. May is the month when the flowers are at their peak and days can be warm enough for the beach.

Details about Cornwall have faded in my mind over the years. We didn't go about as tourists collecting information. I have more recently jogged some memories with promotional literature on the place. Cornwall is the most southwest region of England. Its extreme western part is called Lands End. The region is perhaps the most habitable in England for the summer fun of boating, sunning, and even swimming. The town of Penzance is notable in this regard.

Weather permitting, vacationers repose on deck chairs facing the ocean and the sun, fully clothed when clouds obstruct the sun. When the clouds part, a mad scramble ensues while shirts (only) are removed. They go back on if clouds move in. I suppose this is an instinctive reaction meant to buttress stores of vitamin D.

Cornwall is steeped in history. Until 200 years ago, residents spoke a Celtic language of their own. Phoenicians searching for tin were the first to land there, some 2000 years ago. King Arthur with his Knights of the Round Table founded a castle on the rocky cliffs of Tintagel. Carol and I had a drink at the historic Jamaica Inn, which is also the title of a famous book by Daphne duMaurier.

I must admit that Carol was not my exclusive companion at dances and elsewhere and certainly not when boozing up at the club or with this purpose in mind at some pub. But the times with her are fondly remembered. Some attempt was made after the war to maintain contact, but this effort gradually declined and ceased when she remarried.

TWO MORE AND A VACATION

A FEW COMMENTS

Missions 7 and 8 are described in this chapter along with a latter day visit with my original pilot, John Belingheri. Number 7 turned out to be terrifying and bloody. Not counting practice missions, flying dates from my first through number 8 were December 2, 4, 6, 12, 24, 29, and 30, and January 1 and 3, 1945. During this period, the group flew a total of 17 missions. The very critical period leading up to the Battle of the Bulge was a period of poor weather. Only one mission was flown in the period of December 12 through 24. From December 24 through January 3, the group flew a mission each and every day. Sometimes there were two missions in a single day when the group was split into two (or more) sub-groups attacking different targets.

Through mission 8, we flew a variety of airplanes, most with nose art and names. These are some that we flew: *Old Ironpants, Wolves, Inc., Li'l Peach, Silver Chief, Honey Wagon,* and *The Perfect Lady.* Other names were *Pappy's Yokum, E Pluribus Aluminum,* and *Mesillo Tiger.* And our own *Gremlin Manor.* A few had no name at all.

I was not privy to the philosophy of scheduling crews for missions. I do not know why we did not fly in the critical period of December 25 through 28. (Recall that December 29 was a nonmission.) After number 8 on January 3, we did not fly combat again until February 21, which was over 6 weeks. The

FIGURE 7-1.   Bomb bursts on Magdeburg. (I did not fly this one.)

reason was somewhat confusing to me and remains so. John, the pilot, always had a quite husky voice and was in and out of the hospital on several occasions. In later life he had operations for cancer of the larynx and muscles in one arm. His physical difficulties may have affected him emotionally as well. We did not always fly with him after February 21, but I no longer have records of all of the pilots that we did fly with. I do have a record that shows that John was our pilot on a mission on April 15, 1945.

Had we not been on nonflying status for 6 weeks (except for practice flying), we would probably have finished our limit of 35 missions well before the end. Maybe inactivity was a blessing in disguise. Otherwise, I might have ended up in Asia guiding a bomber over Okinawa or some other well-defended place. Navigators were still scarce, especially experienced ones.

Mr. Healy's book has a roster of names of those who served some time with the 467th. He admits inability to list all because it was done a couple of years after the end. I am the only officer in my crew that is listed. Except for the engineer, the enlisted men are shown in the book. This probably resulted from the way we returned home after it was over. I flew home with different officers, and all but one of my original enlisted flight crew, plus our entire ground crew. We were still officially in business and headed somewhere. (Guess where!)

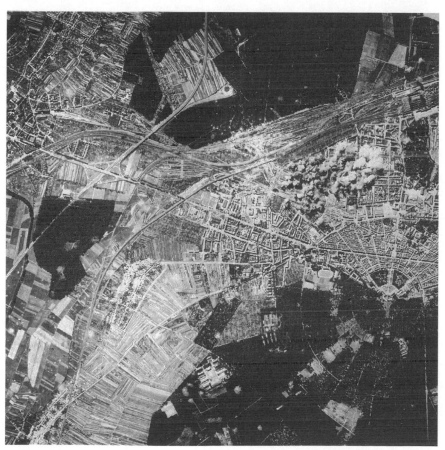

FIGURE 7-2.   Pattern of bursts at Karlsruhe. (I did not fly this one.)

FIGURE 7-3. Crew chief of *Gremlin Manor*.

FIGURE 7-4.   Author right, pilot middle, Winfield left.

Healy's book was reprinted but not by Mr. Healy. The last printing, in 1993, contains an addendum in which the other officers of my crew are listed, but without addresses.

MEETING THE PILOT

I remembered that our pilot was from Pioche, Nevada. How could one forget that name! In 1992, I attended an electronics convention in Las Vegas with my wife, Rita. We took the opportunity to drive to Pioche to do some "snooping." The town is about 140 miles slightly east of north from Las Vegas and about 30 miles from the Utah border. It was winter, and the high desert was blanked with a thin layer of snow. The sight was something to stir the soul. We finally got to Pioche, a one-time silver mining town that, like so many others, had seen better days. We found a bar, somewhat suggesting the center of town, and went in to ask questions. As we entered, the patrons suddenly fell silent. Curious glances came from the old guys who had been talking to one another and to the bartender. Brass rail, spittoon, and all. I ordered a cup of coffee so as to give the appearance of sociability. My wife then blurted out: "Hey, we're not from the IRS." Then she explained who we were looking for and why. The customers all brightened up and became our instant friends. "We know John. He is a nice old guy. But he no longer lives here. He moved a few miles down the road to Panaca." Thanking them we got in the car and left. (I didn't want to accept the idea that I was also an old guy, nice or not.)

Panaca, Pioche, and the surrounding area are all fairly high in elevation, around 4000 feet above sea level. Mountain passes between towns often rise above 6000 feet. The little water that comes with rain or snow flows into the ground without any outlets that eventually reach the sea.

Panaca is not on the main (two lane) highway. It sits off a fraction of a mile on the east side. A small airport is west of the highway. These small-town people are more sophisticated than many think, with light aircraft to go to the big city when the mood strikes.

A couple of hundred yards down the main street, we came to a general store. I went in to ask directions. The owner brightened up and said: "Follow me and I'll show you." With that he got into his pickup, leaving the store open and unattended. A few blocks down the road and on a side street, he pointed to a house and waved goodbye.

A gentleman was just getting into a pickup. I approached him. I recognized him, but he did not recognize me. My opening remark was: "Remember your messed up navigator?" This was a term of "identification" that he (alone) used in England. With that, he went all to pieces with excitement, cried, and hugged. Then he dashed inside the house to get his teeth. We went inside, met his wife, and talked. His home is full of war relics and reminders, much more than mine. He had remained in the service for a time but quit when his next assignment was to be North Africa. He got into selling insurance in Las Vegas and earned not one, but two one-million-dollar certificates. His home is quite modest, in keeping with a mining town in the middle of nowhere where crime is almost absent. The couple has lived a full life with four children and some grandchildren.

His throat problems eventually led to having his larynx removed. He used "esophageal speech" through a hole in his lower throat. But otherwise he seemed hale and hearty. Like me, he had not been in contact with any other crew member.

On our return, we were warned about not driving the slightest bit over the speed limit going through the town of Caliente. When we got to this place, a "cop truck" began following us, all the way through town. I guess he was quite disappointed in not catching an obvious tourist in a rented car from the big city. We survived that one. It reminded me of my days at Stanford University and the most famous (or infamous) "Menlo Cop."

I did try to contact John again in 1996 but got no response. Apparently my visit resulted in his continuing to write some of his war memories. John died in November, 1994. I was not aware that he had any written material until I tried again to contact him by phone in March, 1997. His widow answered, told of his death, and expressed pleasure in sending us a copy of his notes. The eight-page, close-spaced, hand-written script shows some decline in writing ability.

MEETING THE COPILOT

After 52 years, I discovered where Vernon O. Mason lives. My wife and I promptly visited with him and his wife at his home in Tacoma, Washington. He had stayed in the service, but not as a pilot. Rather, he served as a maintenance officer, traveling to far-off places such as Alaska, Japan, Korea, and elsewhere. He retired as a (young) major and thereafter continued his maintenance career up to final retirement.

During our visit, he surveyed the manuscript of this book in search of errors, omissions, lies, and so forth. Only one item was challenged, and this might be a matter of interpretation. He recalls the name of our plane was *Old Ironpants, The Perfect Lady*. We flew in this plane four times plus an abort, compared to two and an abort in *Gremlin Manor*. I prefer *Gremlin Manor* because we created the name and the logo.

There was a waitress at one of the local pubs who had a reputation for avoiding all temptations at love making. Thus the name *Ironpants*!

He clarified something about our bloody nonmission, described previously. To me, logic implied that the engineer did the dirty deed. John Belingheri said it was the tail gunner. Mason said that the engineer had in fact confessed to him that he did it. Makes sense. Maybe the pilot did not issue the order. The engineer and Mason are now my heroes!

He also reminded me of some wild and crazy things that we did together, plus something about my reputation that I knew nothing about. That is, I was recognized as being the fastest G-Man in the group: I could work this navigation device better and faster than anyone else.

Wild things we did? Once after a group party I "stole" the Colonel's bicycle and rode it back to my hut. Not wanting to be accused of pilferage, I (we) moved it to another hut and covered over the tracks in the snow.

We "stole" Sir Edward's trees for fuel. And we also stole more than our share of two buckets of coke per week. On one occasion we heard voices about the coke supply bin and, without being seen, made comments that appeared to label us as MPs (military police). The other party left very quickly indeed!

Mason had not prepared any written accounts of his experiences. But he had a number of photographs. Some of these are superior in quality to mine (less damaged through carelessness), and I have used them here where possible. I also have included some of his original photos, which I did not have.

MISSION NUMBER 7: JANUARY 1, 1945, KOBLENZ, GERMANY

This one to Koblenz (or Coblenz) in the Rhur Valley was a quite frightening one. This valley was (is) Germany's principal region for industrial production. It was New Year's day. We had four 2000-pound giants on board. The target was a bridge over the Moselle River where it empties into the Rhine. The bombs were labeled in chalk: "Happy New Year."

The thing that made this mission especially frightening was that the bomb run was into the teeth of a 130-knot head wind. Our ground speed was only 80 knots, and the bomb run was 37 miles long. Plenty of time to pray. What made it even worse was that we flew somewhat lower than usual at under 20,000 feet. Bombing accuracy increases at lower altitudes, but so does the accuracy of antiaircraft fire!

What happened on the bomb run? Flak was very accurate. We saw two of our ships go down. One had an engine on fire. Another got hit in the flight deck, setting off all of the flares. A few men bailed out from this one, but the damned Germans tracked them in their parachutes with their damned flak! A P-38 attacked us but broke off before firing. Either the Germans had one, or else we mistook one of theirs for one of our own designs. A group of 8 ME 109s also attacked us but broke off at 800 yards when headlight tracers came at them, again illustrating how firepower in close formation could discourage them from continuing. Had they pressed their attack, we would most likely have lost a couple more ships. The mission started with 29 planes. Seven did not return. We hoped that at least some of these were able to find emergency facilities.

Every plane that went on this mission had at least one hole in it, some as many as 50. Several purple hearts resulted over and above crew deaths. We had two sizable holes. Had one large piece been a few inches higher, we would have needed a new copilot. I dug a piece of steel out of my desk. I was thankful that it didn't damage my maps. The past week had cost 12 ships and 40 known deaths, plus missing and/or missing and presumed dead. I suspect that some of the names in Allan Healy's listing of missing in action belong to the killed-in-action category because the list was compiled after the end of hostilities and presumably well after living prisoners had been repatriated.

We got moderate but accurate flak approaching the target for 5 seemingly endless minutes, and another 5 minutes near our front lines going out. On the slow bomb run, we (our ship only) did an unorthodox thing. Although we were all frightened by flak, our pilot might have been even more so. A group of four flak bursts appeared off of our left wing. The pilot "instinctively" veered to the right. The same four bursts followed us, just off of our left wing. Eventually separation from the main group became so large as to invite an air attack. So the pilot banked and headed back toward the formation. Wouldn't you know it, but the same four bursts now appeared just off of our right wing and followed us for a time! Clearly, we were in the gunner's cross hairs. What if Lt. Belingheri had not veered away from the main formation? At least we got back soon enough to complete the bomb run, and by then the four bursts had stopped.

We destroyed the bridge, an important railway link to Germany's front lines. It just goes to show what one can do with a total of 4 times 29, or 116, 1-ton bombs! As a result, it then took 5 to 8 days for Germans to reach the front from the Koln (Calogne) area. This was the eighth straight day of bombing the German supply lines to Runstead's salient.

MISSION NUMBER 8: JANUARY 3, 1945, ZWEIBRUCKEN, GERMANY

This was not nearly as rough as number 7. The target was a railway marshalling yard. It was bombed by radar because cloud cover was 10/10 (complete undercast) both going in and coming out. We carried 20, 250-pound general-purpose bombs and two 500-pound M-17 incindiary clusters. Flak was at the target, but it stopped just before we got there. We were a bit nervous when one of the M-17s hung up in the bomb rack. We had to bring it all the way back, which we did by flying alone under the overcast. We carried an RCM operator. What did he do? He had equipment that listens for German radar and then sends out jamming noise in order to make the radar ineffective. The mission was important because the Germans had just started a drive in the Saarbrucken area, and we wanted to cut their supply lines before they got a good start. They had cut 5 miles into our lines before our raids. The drive was stopped.

PILOT COMMENTS ON TAKEOFFS AND FORMATIONS

John's memoirs are quite sketchy on matters concerning actual combat. However, he does describe some procedures and some difficult situations involving flying in and under clouds. His comments follow (with some editing). My comments are in brackets:

> The crew checked out their stations. Copilot and I checked the bird outside and inside and the flight log. Bombardier and navigator each checked their stations. From the tower a flare would be fired which told us to get aboard. A little later another flare of a different color appeared and that meant to start the engines. [*Note:* Flares were used so as to maintain radio silence.]
>
> Starting the engines was quite a procedure. You would start #2 [inboard right side]. The reason for this was that it had the generator to charge the batteries to start the other three. The put-put turned over its own generator to make electricity for starting #2 engine. Making sure that the put-put was in ready order was the engineer's duty—check oil, gas, and starter. The put-put was located just forward of the bomb bays.
>
> The next flare meant to taxi for takeoff. Each procedure flare had a different color which we knew. We were to taxi out in a certain sequence and so we would sit in the hardstand until the ship number meant to precede us went by and then we would follow. [Planes arrived at the end of the runway from two directions, and the takeoff sequence would have them leave like shuffling cards.] Another flare would be shot off and #1 would take off. We took off one every 30 seconds [by the watch]. Twenty-nine or 31 was acceptable but less or more and you answered to the brass that night.
>
> The way we timed our takeoff [when you are in position] starts with the pilot pushing all four throttles fully forward while he and the copilot both hold the toe brakes. The navigator would be behind the pedestal between the pilot and copilot with his stop watch. At 5 seconds before the half minute mark he would start counting down. On the word "go" we would release the brakes and start down the runway. The runways were around 5000 feet long, just enough to get off. But with a big load, we often would haul back to get off before we met with the fence.

After assembly, a group of [usually] three squadrons would be arranged in a certain configuration. The high squadron would have two groups of 3 planes plus another 3 above and to the right. The middle or main group would have two sets of 3 planes and 3 more below and to the right. The lower squadron would have two sets of 3 and 3 more above and to the right. This gave 27 aircraft in groups of 9. The best [safest from ground fire] would be the high element in the high squadron. To get there, you had to have seniority! We called the lowest 3 "coffin corner" and 3 of the main body "purple heart corner." This was because the heavy shells coming up from the ground were usually aimed at the main body and had to go through you to get there. At night we would form up in the same manner but sometimes the sky was bright with fire from a midair collision.

PILOT COMMENTS ON GOING TO AND FROM A TARGET

As soon as we cleared the English shoreline our gunners would test fire their guns in the sea to make sure they were in working order. From then on you were "sitting ducks" to flak and enemy fighters. We had a good escort when we had the P-51 with us, but we didn't think too much of the P-47. It just didn't give us the cover we wanted. When we hit our IP [the point where we started our bomb run] we closed our formation as tight as we could and we couldn't make any moves to avoid flak. The bomb run had to be straight and level in order to hit the target.

Enemy fighters would not attack us when the flak was coming up. When the ground fire wanted to tell fighters to move in, they would fire a few bursts of red colored flak.

After "bombs away" we would make a sharp turn and head for home and hope we would get there. On a clear day we just followed the lead ship in formation and went to the field. The bottom ships would pitch off first and again we would have 30-second intervals on our landings. If we were too long we would have to go right back up and shoot a set number of practice landings. This didn't go over very well after you had been in the air for a bunch of hours fighting the elements and the cold. We were usually hungry and tired as hell. We wore electric suits, but they didn't always work. One glove would go out and you would sit on the bad one in hopes your butt would keep the hand warm. There also was a hidden (more or less) camera in some of the planes taking pictures of the formation. If you were flying a bad formation you would get to fly a bunch of practice missions over England. No mission credit for these joy rides.

PILOT COMMENTS ON INSTRUMENT LETDOWNS

If the weather was bad and you had to make an instrument letdown, it was quite a deal. You would be above the overcast and so you would tune in on a weak radio station on the coast. Our field was about 25 miles inland. When above the clouds and over the water we would home in on the radio signal. When we were directly over the radio we could tell this by either audio or the radio compass. We would then turn away from the coast and begin a letdown through the clouds at a rate of descent of 500 to 1000 feet per minute. We would go out one minute for every 1000 feet of altitude that we lost and then make a 180 degree turn so as to head back towards the radio. We would break out of the overcast before we got back to the shore. You could usually figure a ceiling of 50 to 100 feet over the water. It was always a welcome sight to see the shore. When over the radio at low altitude we would continue our inbound heading until we came to a railroad track. Then we would follow the track until it became two tracks and we took the one on the left. It led to the runways of your field. Then everyone on board would be on the lookout for other planes while we were in the traffic pattern.

The instrument approach method was good. However in England the weather could and would change in just a few minutes and you could be blinded by clouds [fog] and lose the railroad tracks. Wander left or right and at 50 feet a small rise in the ground with a high object would be the end. Occasionally you might see the clouds light up and you would know that some plane had hit something. Church steeples were bad objects for this.

How would you find your way over England at night? The country was covered by many weak radio stations with a range of only about 25 miles. Each had a separate call number but the same frequency. Calling got the one closest to you. His call signal would then tell you roughly where you were, and you could be directed back to your own base. A system of lights would direct you to the runway once you were close enough to see them.

GERMAN WEAPONS AND MORE MISSIONS

MISSION NUMBER 9: FEBRUARY 21, 1945, NURNBERG, GERMANY

This mission was the first we flew after almost 6 weeks of peace and quiet (except for practice missions, ground school, etc., etc.). Manufacturing plants and marshalling yards were targets. The whole 8th Air Force descended upon these places. The weather was clear as we passed into enemy territory. Flak was moderate but accurate on the way, and it resulted in a big bang and a hole in the airplane. The sky then turned undercast. We got more moderate but accurate flak at the target with three bursts directly under us. Three men in other aircraft got purple hearts on this mission, and there was considerable damage to most aircraft. But all managed to return safely. We expected more intense flak than we actually got. Our load was 10 500-pound, general-purpose bombs. Air time was 8 hours. This was the second day in a row that this particular target was hit.

MISSION NUMBER 10: FEBRUARY 22, 1945, HILDESHEIM, GERMANY

The marshalling yard was the target including rail equipment and cars. The entire 8th Air Force was after similar targets as were the 9th (twin-engine attack aircraft), fighter groups, and the 15th out of Italy. The intent was to isolate the Rhur Valley, the largest industrial area in Germany, from the rest of the country. This task had an enhanced importance because Selesia, another heavy industrial town, had fallen to the Russians. The Rhur area had become Germany's only remaining large region with the factories needed to make tanks and heavy artillery.

In order to achieve maximum damage, we did something "crazy" by bombing from only 7000 feet above the ground! We climbed to 18,000 on the way in and out in order to minimize danger from flak. About two-thirds of the way in, we dropped to 8500 feet (above sea level). At the wing initial point, flak was moderate and very accurate. How we escaped with only three holes, I'll never know. Each burst was a big bang that rocked the ship, none over 100 feet away. Everything was thrown at us, not only 88 mm but also 40 mm. One of our ships got its wing shot off, and it crashed. No chutes were seen. One plane came back 514 miles on only two engines. Several more came back on three. We flew deputy lead back because the original left formation due to battle damage. The group got a couple more purple hearts.

Although out of character, I really prayed today for our crew. But there was a reward as well because we had a front row seat to view in detail how the target was destroyed. This mission was the most frightening thus far. The stress was so great that I actually smoked on the bomb run (no oxygen needed). Was this relaxation, or was it a reaction from terror? We saw no one looking at us, but we did see even machine guns trying to reach us.

The bomb load was 12, 500-pound GPs. Airborne time was 7 hours. On this mission, our usual pilot was in the hospital. He was replaced by Lt. Sullivan.

COMMENTS ON GERMAN WEAPONS

In visual weather, altitude above the ground can be judged well enough to direct the trajectory of a shell fired from a German gun on the ground. The shell is timed to explode

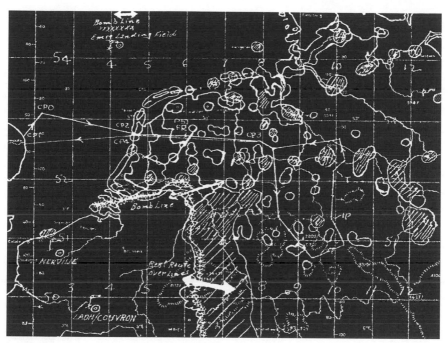

FIGURE 8-1.   Route chart to Hildesheim.

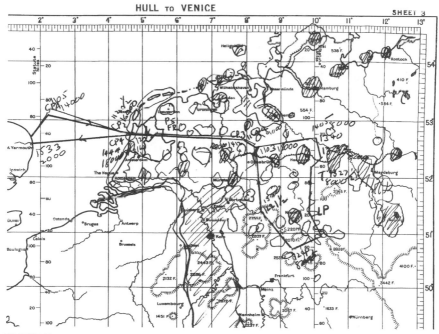

FIGURE 8-2.   Navigator's chart to Hildesheim.

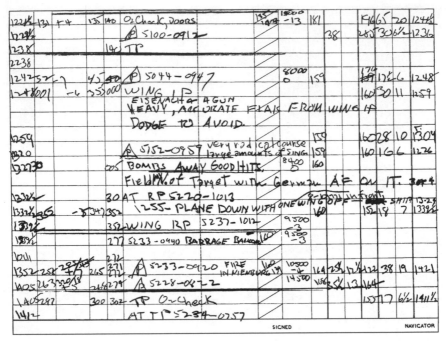

FIGURE 8-3. Part of navigator's log to Hildeshieim. (Age has darkened the paper and smeared the writing.)

when it reaches the proper altitude. This timing process is not accurate enough to always get within a lethal distance above or below the aircraft. Multiple salvos help to adjust the altitude measure, which means that the longer you are exposed to flak, the more accurate it can become. Slow bomb runs are murder!

During World War II, we developed the *proximity fuse.* Our antiaircraft shells contained a little radio transmitter that could sense a fairly large nearby metal object. The method was to detect a change in antenna loading, roughly similar to an echo effect. This invention was important in our air war in the Pacific. Fortunately for us, the Germans did not have this "smart" fuse. If they had, we might not have been able to continue our intense daylight bombing program. If the Germans couldn't see us through an overcast, their gun laying accuracy, set by radar, even without jamming and chaff, was rather inaccurate. Our bombing accuracy was similarly compromised.

When we couldn't see each other, the fight was like one between blind warriors.

As an aside, consider our present-day "stealth" aircraft. These purport to be invisible to radar. But what about a proximity fuse? If they represent a large mass of metal, the mass will interact with a transmitting coil to detune it slightly. This is all that a proximity fuse based on this principle needs.

The German weapon that we feared most was the ME 262 jet fighter, the first ever to go into combat anywhere. Had the Germans emphasized their jet program earlier and possessed more of them, I don't think we could have continued with daylight bombing. An attacking jet did not fly a normal pursuit curve. Rather, it would fly through the formation in a way that denied our gunners a fair chance for getting a hit. Each fly-through could result in a destroyed bomber. When the powers-that-be recognized the seriousness of this problem, increased

FIGURE 8-4.   Exploding munitions train at Hildesheim.

emphasis by some elements of the 8th Air Force was given to the bombing of aircraft manufacturing plants, oil storage facilities, and airfields where jets might be located. Pock-marked runways cannot be used, at least for a short time.

These early jets did have a weakness. Their endurance was limited by a high rate of fuel consumption, which meant that, after an attack or two, a quick and partly gliding return to base was necessary. The landing field often turned out to be a stretch of the autobahn highway system. Our fighter pilots could destroy these jets if they could follow them to their landing places. The jets had too little fuel to outrun our propeller-driven ships during a partly gliding return to their home bases. Even though coming late in the war, one account states that these jets downed 600 of our bombers.

There was yet another remarkable German weapon. It was a true rocket plane, the ME 263. Performance of this was awesome, getting to altitude in little more than a minute. But time under power was much shorter than the jets. Their very high speed worked against having enough time to pump many bullets into our aircraft. Also they were made very light in weight and could not carry an array of many machine guns and small cannons projecting from the wings. Not many of these ever became fully operational. Like the jet, it was a matter of too little and too late for the Germans. Returning to base was strictly a gliding process, which made these rocket planes even more vulnerable to our fighters, if they could be seen well enough to be followed.

We must give the Germans lots of credit for their engineering. They pioneered the now standard delta wing design. To this day the ME 263 remains the only rocket plane that ever saw combat and the only rocket plane that flew on a regular basis.

The Germans also pioneered with pulse jet pilotless aircraft, the V-1, which caused much damage in and about London. They also created the V-2 rocket. We captured some of their rocket scientists. The Russians captured many as well, possibly ending up with more than we had. Both we and the Russians created and developed our own missile technologies on the backs of these captured scientists and engineers. The most illustrious on our side was Werner von Braun.

It so happens that I have considerable personal knowledge of our early missile work. After completing a couple of degrees in electrical engineering at Stanford University, I went to work at the Jet Propulsion Laboratory of the California Institute of Technology. We were developing the guidance system for the Corporal missile, which eventually became our country's very first guided ballistic missile. I had the privilege of designing a considerable part of the ground-based guidance system, including a most critical part that shut off the fuel when the rocket reached a calculated speed. If timing was right, the rocket would have the correct range. The measurement was of speed based on the Doppler frequency shift phenomenon. The idea came from a somewhat similar device that the Germans had begun to install in their V-2s. (Some of my notes and technical reports have been donated to the Smithsonian Institution.)

We didn't just design and build our rocket gadgets. We also traveled to White Sands Proving Grounds and shot them off! In those days the entire staff of the guidance and control group numbered less than a handful of degreed engineers! White Sands is the place where Dr. von Braun worked.

MISSION NUMBER 11: FEBRUARY 26, 1945, EBERSWALDE, GERMANY

The target was a marshalling yard in the heart of the city of Berlin. This was for convenience only. The idea was to cause as much confusion and damage as possible. Our group messed up on this one. The clouds were 10/10 undercast. Our radar operator was having trouble with interplane communications. We flew all over Berlin looking for holes in the clouds. We even thought of making a 360 degree turn over the target for a second try. In looking at the considerable flak around us, we thought that a target outside the central part of the city would be a better choice. So we finally bombed a small town,

Eberswalde, on the outskirts of Berlin. This place corresponded to the wing's rallying point (where we were scheduled to go
after dropping on the preferred target). The bomb load was six
500-pound bombs and four M17 incindiary clusters.

Our ship got four large holes and had to go to the sub
depot for major repairs. One piece messed up the left aileron.
A huge chunk narrowly missed the right tire and then nearly
severed the right main wing spar. Another piece went into the
junction box coolers of number 3 engine and then into a fuel
cell. We were indeed lucky that the ship did not catch fire and
blow up! As it was, our right wing vibrated and swayed in a
frightening manner all the way home because of the nearly
severed main spar. We were lucky to keep it.

With all this damage, I still observed in my original black
book that flak was not nearly as bad as anticipated and that
our group was lucky because we got less of the stuff than any
other group.

Still, four ships did not return. Hopefully they made it to
France because of insufficient fuel to return to England. But I
don't know. We were in the air for 8½ hours and bombed from
23,000 feet. Winds were strong, giving us a ground speed
of 90 knots on the way out. This is about the speed of a
Cessna 150 in still air. We feared the German Air Force (GAF)
because our escort left us at Dummer Lake.

It is interesting in retrospect to read my comments to the
effect that flak was not as severe as expected even though we
were getting shot to hell. A kind of psychological "detach-
ment" is demonstrated.

A MID-MARCH NIGHTMARE

Our group went again to Berlin in mid-March. I was not on
this one. Three out of 27 ships were lost over the target,
which is over 10 percent in a single mission. The historian
Allan Healy cites this as one of the roughest missions the
group ever flew. Clearly, the Germans were not yet through. A
lead plane piloted by Lt. Chapman was hit and left the forma-

tion with limited control. The deputy lead took over, but time was inadequate to get good results from the bombs that were dropped. Another plane was shot down, but it still managed a perfect bomb pattern on the target.

Lt. Chapman's navigator was killed by a hit in his head. The engineer was blown to bits as he squatted to watch the bombs away. A fire in the bomb bay was extinguished by the wind entering a hole smashed in the nose. On two engines, the plane was brought under control and headed for the Russian lines some 40 miles away. An ME 109 was driven off by Russian Yak fighters, which then proceeded to fire at the hapless B-24. By then, only one engine was working, and altitude was being lost at the rate of 1500 feet per minute. The remaining crew bailed out beyond the lines and were shot at in their

FIGURE 8-5. Pattern of first squadron's bombs cover one target in Berlin. Bright spots to left are first explosions of second squadron's bombs directly on second target.

FIGURE 8-6.   Complete pattern of second squadron's bombs.

chutes by the Russian Yaks, and then from the ground by Russian riflemen. They were captured and roughed up until one crew member, who knew Polish, yelled "Ya Amerikanets." The vodka then came out and all were friendly. As I recall, Lt. Chapman was our pilot on a mission that John Belingheri did not make.

This incident, and many more of a similar nature, left many of us with a sour taste for Russians. As I recall, near the end of hostilities, more than a few of us were in favor of continuing right on to Moscow. It's just a good thing we didn't do this. The bulk of German might was trying to stave off the Russians. Maybe Germans were fighting us and the British and the French with one hand tied behind their back. Russia prevailed because they were willing to sacrifice untold numbers of their own fighters. Could we have prevailed over such an enemy without using "the bomb"?

MISSION NUMBER 12: FEBRUARY 28, 1945, BIELEFELD, GERMANY

This one went to the same bridge we had repeatedly missed before. The mission was entirely uneventful. It was a complete milk run with no flak and no fighters. There were occasional breaks in the clouds, but the undercast was complete at the target. Bombing was by radar. Again we missed the target, probably exacting an even larger toll on civilians. The bomb load was six 1000-pound GPs, and air time was 7 hours.

MISSION NUMBER 13: MARCH 1, 1945, INGOLSTADT, GERMANY

I am not a superstitious person. Nevertheless, I list this mission as "number 12b" in my little black book. Our target was a plant making parts for jet planes, and we were to hit it only if it was visual. Our secondary target, to be hit by radar if the primary was not visual (which it was not), was the marshalling yard in the same city. The load was 10 500-pound bombs, and flying time was 9½ hours. We flew clear around Munich. This was a long mission for an important but small target which, unfortunately, we were not able to bomb. No flak and no fighters for our squadron, but all of us sweat gas. Another squadron did get some flak, and one crew member was killed. Several planes did not return, most probably in France for gas. The time in the air was considerably longer than average.

On March 2, 1945, the group went to Magdeburg. We were not on this one. One plane and crew gone.

MISSION NUMBER 14: MARCH 3, 1945, NIENBERG AND BIELEFELD, GERMANY

The target was an important railroad bridge to be hit visually if possible. The radar alternative was the marshalling yard at

Bielefeld (again). We carried six 1000-pound bombs and were airborne for $7\frac{1}{4}$ hours.

The lead squadron hit the target really well, and the bridge was destroyed. We were the second squadron, but clouds obscured the target. Our particular ship toggled on the lead plane's smoke markers because a turbo on one engine failed, and we lost all power in that engine (as if it was not super-charged, but still running). Ours was the only plane in our squadron that did drop on the primary, and we came pretty close.

In order that the rest of our squadron and the third squadron could get a chance to hit the primary target, another hour and a half was spent in the area with four more bomb runs being made, none of which turned out to be visual. Our group was leading the wing. The other groups were moaning about spending so much time in the area. Lack of fighter support made cruising about just a little dangerous.

At last we went to the secondary, Bielefeld, by radar. What we did there was not clearly observed because of the numerous clouds and general confusion. No doubt, the civilian population suffered.

There were no fighters, but there was some flak. Upon our return, we had the distressing task of removing the belongings of our hut buddies. The commanding officer had the task of writing family members.

MISSION NUMBER 15: MARCH 9, 1945, OSNABRUCK, GERMANY

The targets were railroad shops and the marshalling yard. Bomb load was 44 100-pound GPs and two M17 incindiary clusters. The flak was intense and accurate for other squadrons in our group. Our group got moderate but still accurate flak. A large piece bounced off the fuselage and then off the armored glass. On the outside of the cabin next to the pilot, there was installed a sheet of protective steel, which did save many lives. Navigators were not so protected. The mission lasted only 5 hours. I liked these short ones in spite of the flak. One of our planes was lost.

MISSION NUMBER 16: MARCH 11, 1945, KIEL, GERMANY

The target was a shipyard where 70 submarines were presumably being built. Many ships were in the harbor. We carried 52 100-pound M47 jellied gas incindiaries. Flight time was 6 hours. Briefing warned of intense flak for 7 minutes. The flak was there, but it was inaccurate, made so by a screening force of four American-flown mosquito bombers distributing chaff. It was 10/10 over the target with large holes, which made us nervous because this would give the Germans a visual gun-aiming capability.

The total time over Denmark and Germany was only 40 minutes in the 6 hours of the mission. We saw four jet jobs, but they did not attack. Our group led the 8th Air Force. My G box went out just before we started on course. Fortunately the wind was constant enough so that I could use previously computed values. Groups just ahead and just behind our group experienced much more flak than we did. Our luck held because the flak almost stopped for our group! Other groups received considerable damage and lost aircraft.

MORE MISSIONS

I still have a number of missions to describe, from number 17 through 31. This chapter covers about half of these with the rest in the next chapter. The reader may wish to skip over some of them. Getting shot at every day or two can indeed get to be "boring"!

However, I start out this and the next chapter with sections not directly related to my exploits. I let John, the pilot, describe a humorous (noncombat) incident in the next chapter.

A few highlights of the remaining missions are mentioned briefly here. Number 17 was at the request of the Russians, their first such request. Number 21 was bad for other groups, but we escaped. Number 22 had attacks by ME 262s (jets). We saw planes go down on number 23, but not from our squadron. Number 25 set the 8th Air Force record for bombing accuracy by a single bomb group (ours). On number 28 we bombed Czechoslovakia. Number 29 gave us the record for accuracy of a single bomb squadron (ours). Number 30 had a scary return under low clouds while steering around church steeples in Germany and France. Number 31, the last flown by the 8th Air Force, was at the request of General Patton.

THE BEST GROUP

It was not until I read Allan Healy's book that I realized that our bomb group stood at the head of its class, not only in the entire Second Division of the 8th Air Force but for all of the other divisions (B-17s) as well. Indeed, we sometimes missed targets and schedules. But so did others, more so than we. Our objectives were measured on a day-to-day basis, and most of us did not know how we ranked with our peers. All we could do was our best and, whenever possible, accept practice missions with grace.

We had the lowest loss rate in the entire division. This was no doubt partly the result of practice and a virtual obsession with precision flying. Briefing came after considerable study aimed at avoiding flak regions other than at the intended target and to maintain planes to the highest possible standards. Maintenance really was good. On Christmas Eve, we flew every plane on the field, and only one had to abort. You can count 50 in the formation that was photographed. My own 789th Bomb Squadron flew a record 201 consecutive missions without a single aircraft aborted.

It is not without a little sense of guilt that I must admit that my own aircraft ended this string with two aborted flights in a single day, March 23, 1945. We were supposed to go to Osnabruck, Germany. We barely got off the ground and could not get our gear up. We were forced to abort in *Gremlin Manor*. We went quickly to the spare loaded with incendiary clusters and took off late. Just as we joined the formation, 5 minutes from the CPI, we lost practically all power in engine number 1, and oil spewed out in gross quantities. We were forced to abort in this ship as well, losing all power in the engine just as we landed. The cause was a blown cylinder. The engine on our second ship had over 300 hours on it, and the crew chief said he expected it to fail but could not get a new one. As a result, three new ones were put on. The mission? They got shot up quite a bit with all but two aircraft having flak damage. A couple of purple hearts were "earned." We did not go far enough on this mission to get shot at, and so we did not get credit for it.

There were records not related to flying as well. The motor pool had the lowest accident rate. The photo section set the pace of the division with its skills, and our "Airliners" band won the division contest. A crew chief by the name of Held received commendation for the best kept aircraft in the division. A 30-hour engine change was done in 8.5 hours. Rackheath was an especially well-kept base with full military atmosphere of spit and polish (albeit, things got a bit relaxed at party time).

It was bombing results that really set us apart. What percentage of bombs from a group fall within the 1000-foot circle about the aiming point? The 500-foot circle? Indeed, other measures of destruction might have been defined, but these measures were the best we could construct when bombing was at 18,000 feet and above without benefit of follow-up analysis on the ground.

A paper called *Target Victory* was published by the second division. This paper reported on attacks and their successes. Before I joined the group in November, 1944, it had been up and down in credits but usually first or second in the wing. From early November on, our group was always at the top of the list! On April 14, we scored 100 percent in 1000 feet and 58 percent in 500 feet for an all-time bombing accuracy record for the entire 8th Air Force. I was on that mission. We dropped 1-ton bombs (four per plane) on the casement coastal battery at Point de Grave, France, along the fortified approaches to the Bordeaux harbor. The bombing record for a single squadron was set on my 29th mission on April 20. My squadron got all of its bombs in the 500-foot circle except for a couple on the edge.

But there was more. We consistently led in percent of aircraft fully operational, and we were first or second for many months in lowest losses. We did not always have the lowest combat crew losses but were usually among the lowest. Most of the time we had the fewest mechanical failures in the division, and the number of aircraft making effective sorties was high.

The first 100 missions (before I joined the group) were completed in only 140 days—another record. When the war ended (last mission April 25, 1945), the group had flown 212 missions using 5105 aircraft sorties. We had dropped 13,353 tons of bombs with 35,537 hours of operational flying time.

We lost 49 aircraft plus many more that were damaged beyond repair. We used a total of 160 combat B-24s.

We did experience some attacks by fighters, but fewer of these than other groups owing to our tight formations. Gunners bagged five planes, ME 109s and FW 190s, plus some damaged ones. ("Damage" is the term used if you don't actually see the plane come apart or crash.)

Allan Healy quotes a letter from the wing commander to Col. Shower:

> The records clearly indicate the continuous outstanding performance of the 467th Group in all phases of operation. Most commendable is the absence of any slumps in your bombing records. You have been at or near the top throughout. It is proof of initiative, tenacity of purpose, and drive exercised by you and your command.

After VE Day, a giant show-off parade of the 8th Air Force flew in formation across High Wycombe and General Doolittle's headquarters. Our 467th was in the lead position.

SONGS OF THE 467TH BOMB GROUP

In the midst of mayhem, we created diversions of all sorts that were humorous or fun (like boozing and chasing). One of our pastimes was to sing "our" songs. Here are three of them, two of which are "nice." I recall only part of one more containing the phrase "Pratt Whitney all over my chest."

RACKHEATH AGGIES   (Tune: "On Wisconsin")

Rackheath Aggies, Rackheath Aggies, out to do or die
Rackheath Aggies, Rackheath Aggies, blundering through the sky.
Our formations are sensations, we're not easily cowed.
We'll drop our bombs until those fields are plowed.

AFTER THE MISSION   (Tune: "After the Ball Is Over")

After the mission's over, after we all get back,
We get interrogated, "Where did you see the flak?"

"How were the German fighters, when were your bombs away,
Do you have any bitches? That's all for today."
We like the Liberator. We think it handles swell.
We like to fly formation, we're just as nuts as Hell.
We like the fithter peel-off, it'll kill us all some day
Land in thirty seconds or Al will have to say.
"Condry, you straggled all day, Tibbetts showed poor technique.
Houston, you had your head up, we'll have a short critique.
You missed the D.A.L., Jones. Johnson, you will report,
Why you thought that one wing off was reason to abort."

TO BERLIN   (Tune: "Wreck of Old '97")

It's a long rough ride from Rackheath to Berlin, and the flak was
  bursting high.
The P-38s and the P-47s were guarding us high up in the sky.
We were halfway between Lake Dummer and Hamburg when all
  hell broke loose in the blue,
For Jerry had spotted us from 5 o'clock under and was coming up
  to see what he could do.
Now the first pass was made at the 467th, Col. Shower was there
  in the lead.
And he pissed and he moaned, and he shit and he groaned, when
  he looked 'round and found he was alone.
So the colonel called to his brave navigator, "Give me a short
  heading home."
But with his hand on the ripcord, he looked back at the colonel
  and said, "Al, boy, you're going home alone."
Then the colonel called to his bombardier, "Can you find the right
  way home?"
But the bombardier had already scuttled, there was silence on the
  colonel's interphone.
With his crew all gone, he chewed on his mustache and his balls
  drew up in his sack.
Oh, he choked on his candy at 22,000 for he never thought that
  he was coming back.
But with 4 engines feathered, he glided it safely to the runways of
  his home base.
And 'tis with much pride that he tells this story, with a shit eatin'
  grin on his face.

MISSION NUMBER 17: MARCH 12, 1945, SWINEMUNDE, GERMANY

Our targets were docks, shipping, and supplies. Also included were warships and the *Admiral Schear* battleship in particular. Bomb load was five 1000-pound GPs. Time in the air was 7:40. At this time, the target was only 12 miles from the Russian lines, and the Reds, for the first time, requested our 8th Air Force to hit a specific target. The route to the target area was mostly visual, but shortly before the initial point it turned 10/10 undercast. There was a great deal of flak over the target, but thanks to our screening force of chaff-dropping American mosquito aircraft, it was all wild for our group. Some groups ahead and behind us were not so lucky. After bombs away, we could look back and see huge boiling clouds of black smoke pouring thousands of feet above the 12,000-foot undercast. There was a great deal of shipping in the Baltic and several large ships north of Kiel. We also observed German submarines. We could see shipping at Heligoland. When we returned, S2 said that they thought we would surely be hit by fighters. It's a good thing we weren't because even Sweden was some distance away. I think that we did a good job.

MISSION NUMBER 18: MARCH 19, 1945, LEIPHEIM, GERMANY

The bomb load was 10 500-pound GPs. The mission was a long one, lasting $8\frac{1}{2}$ hours. Our wing went to this number 1 priority target. It was an assembly plant producing about 100 aircraft per month. We were to bomb it only visually. If undercast, we were to bomb the center of some small town. The weather was clear at the target. I watched our group's bombs and another's incendiaries hit the target. All three of our squadrons hit the target 100 percent in 2000 feet, 85 percent in 1000 feet, and 35 percent in 500 feet (as told to us after S2 analysis). The fire bombs from another group then hit the target and blanketed it to look like millions of sparks covering the area. This was a beautiful job, the prettiest I have ever seen, and the plant was quite thoroughly destroyed. There were a couple of jet jobs on the runways.

This mission was unusual because we formed over the continent at Liege, the second time the division did this and my first. On the way back, we paralleled the Rhine and saw Koblenz, the bridgehead, and Koln. There was a great deal of activity at every point along this river with many smoke screens. Every German town was almost completely leveled where we had conquered. The French and Belgian cities were not nearly so badly beat up. It just goes to prove that every inch we took in Germany had to be blasted loose of Germans; a real bloody and difficult job. The southern front around Strassbourg looked very quiet and inactive, but every bridge was blown down. No flak and no fighters on this mission. I was surprised as we expected flak at the target. At our bombing altitude of 19,000 feet, flak could have been quite effective. We flew in the *Gremlin Manor*.

MISSION NUMBER 19: MARCH 21, 1945, HESEPE AIRFIELD, GERMANY

Bomb load 52, 100-pound GPs and flying time of 5 hours. This airfield was to be bombed visually in order to pock-mark the field and destroy any jets that might be on it. Also, we wanted to destroy small antiaircraft guns so that our fighters could go in and strafe the field relatively safely. The day was beautiful and perfectly visual. The bombing job was very well done.

The entire air force had similar targets in the general area. Our target was near Osnabruck. After we went over the target, a terrific barrage was sent up before us near Osnabruck, but by quick turning, we were able to avoid it. The groups that got into the barrage were hit heavily. I could see more planes today than I ever saw before. No fighters and no battle damage, making this another milk run.

On March 23, we were to bomb the railroad yards at Osnabruck. This was the mission that we had to abort (twice) and so did not fly it. Those that did go got badly shot up with all but 2 of the aircraft having flak damage, 10 of them with major damage. There also were a few purple hearts.

MISSION NUMBER 20: MARCH 24, 1945, KIRTORF, GERMANY

This was another one where we carried 52 100-pound bombs. The flight lasted 6 hours. Our pilot was in the hospital, and we flew with Lt. Sullivan as his replacement. Our group put up two separate missions for the first time since August. We flew the slot. We had just established a new bridgehead across the Rhine, and the aim of our mission (the second one of the day) was to neutralize this airfield for as little as one night because night fighters from this field were giving the ground troops a lot of trouble. The bombing was again excellent with practically all in 2000 feet with an intervelometer setting of 100 feet. We did get a few bursts of inaccurate flak at the rally point and a few on the lines coming out. But there was no battle damage, and we considered this to be a milk run.

MISSION NUMBER 21: MARCH 30, 1945, WILHELMSHAVEN, GERMANY

The bomb load was eight 1000-pound GPs. Flight time was 6 hours. Our target was a parts assembly plant for U-boats, docking facilities, and the battle cruiser *Koln*. We received flak going in but no damage. As we approached the target, we saw a huge barrage of intense flak, mostly large stuff. The group just ahead of us lost three planes in this barrage. For some reason, just as we got to the target, they stopped shooting and threw it up again at the group behind us. Why we never got the hell shot out of us I'll never know. They were probably handing out the cigars! Cloud cover was about six-tenths of cumulus. We bombed from 22,300 feet. The remainder of the trip was uneventful.

MISSION NUMBER 22: APRIL 4, 1945, PERLEBERG, GERMANY

Bomb load was 36 150-pound GPs. The duration of the flight was 7½ hours. The target was an airfield that was to be attacked visually. The pilot was again Lt. Sullivan. The weather was poor, and we thought that we might have to bring our bombs back. We were very much off course the entire mission because of a poor wing lead. We got occasional bursts of meager flak the entire route in. The flak over the target was also meager and not very accurate but must have been 155 mm. On the bomb run, two ME 262s (jets) shot under our formation a couple of hundred feet, and then another attacked our squadron. Every gun in the squadron was trained on him. He might have been firing at us, and we did not see the smoke from his guns. Or maybe for some reason he went right through our formation without firing. Some of the planes did sustain damage, maybe from flak and maybe from the jet. I doubt that we were able to inflict any damage on him. After this, a lone P-51 slid into us, and several of the trigger-happy gunners shot at him. It's a miracle that he wasn't shot down because there were tracers all about him. (It is possible, of course, that the P-51 was one that had been captured earlier by the Germans.)

The rest of the trip was uneventful except for meager flak here and there. Our target was dropped through a very small hole in the clouds after a 70 degree correction in which the lead ship merely toggled, missing the MPI by a mile. This target had 173 planes on it, and we were supposed to knock it out for from 7 to 11 days by post-holing. Even though we did drop and miss by so much, our squadron was the only one in the group that did not bring its bombs back.

As I said, there was some flak. A piece was taken from the nose, 2 feet from me. It was the size of both doubled fists together.

MISSION NUMBER 23: APRIL 9, 1945, LECHFELD, GERMANY

We carried 20 250-pound GPs. Flight time was 8 hours. We were delayed 3 hours on takeoff because of fog. Finally, at 12:30 we did take off. The whole mission was a complete milk run for our squadron although other squadrons in our group received damage. We saw one plane go down over the target and two ditching later in the channel. Again we were lucky because the Hun did not choose to shoot at our particular formation. There was very little activity on the

FIGURE 9-1.   Bomb bursts on Regensburg.

ground that we could see. I had G all the way through the target with the addition of a new chain moved into captured German territory. We were lucky in escaping the flak. Nine bursts and one Liberator down. Very accurate shooting on a perfectly visual day. The ship we flew in was a very windy one and cold and uncomfortable.

MISSION NUMBER 24: APRIL 11, 1945, REGENSBERG, GERMANY

We carried six 1000-pound GPs, and we were airborne 8 hours. Our target was briefed as intense flak. It was an oil storage depot that was one of Hitler's most sorely needed commodities. Since a front had moved in over the base area, we had to assemble at Liege on the continent. Everything went well. The mission was visual, but the lead ship did a lot of unnecessary wandering that made navigation difficult. We sweated out the target. We got our intense flak all right, but they must have had grammar school kids firing the guns because they couldn't hit their nose with both hands. Indeed, this was a most relieving situation. The rest of the mission was uneventful. Both squadrons in our group did excellent bombing. Black smoke poured high in the air as we left. No battle damage.

TO THE END

The final few combat missions that I flew, including the last one by the 8th Air Force, are recounted here. But first let me draw from our pilot's memoirs.

RABBITS AND FERRETS

Everything over there was the "King's." The ferret, rabbit, and pheasant were a few of the many and the only ones I cared about. You could eat the rabbits and the pheasants. The ferrets were nice if you had seen almost nothing but Nevada desert.

The best way to catch a rabbit was to get a ferret (a weasel-like animal), then tie a line on his neck, run the rabbit down his hole, and then send the ferret down after him. He would bring the rabbit out and then all you had to do was to get the rabbit away from him.

However, getting the ferret was a problem and so we had few rabbits. We even tried shooting flares (flare gun) down the hole in hopes we would smoke the rabbit out. But this didn't work too well. The flare was so hot it would cook the rabbit and that was the end of that.

Getting a ferret wasn't too hard. He would come up close to the hut and a trail of bread crumbs would bring him in. A rabbit was something in the pot. Just don't get caught. Remember, you were fooling with the "King's" property.

No rabbit or pheasant would mean round steak or Wieners, fried Spam, liver, and cabbage at the mess hall. Fortunately, I liked them all and so I ate well.

> The drinks weren't too good over there. The only whisky we had
> was after a mission at the debriefing table. The English had sev-
> eral beers (no good). They called them mild, mild and bitter,
> and half and half (pronounced by the English holf and holf).
> They had cola but that was for the ladies. Once in a while you
> could catch one of the pubs with gin. At the Officer's Club you
> could get gin and orange or scotch and coke. After a while, you
> would get a taste for it.
>
> The cream was out of this world, but only when the group had
> a big party like our 200 mission party.
>
> When I was in the hospital, the grub was a lot better. I was in 3
> different ones besides the base (sick call with beds).

My comments: I was raised to think that adding coke to
scotch was completely sacrilegious! The cream he talks about
is the famous Devonshire cream. I tasted a lot of this when on
a business trip (with wife) in the early 1960s. The beer is commonly called arf 'n arf, pronounced as one word with three
syllables (with this pronunciation most used by the English
working class). The reference to the "king's" property is not
quite correct. The animals were part of "Sir Edward's" property. Taking animals from lands owned by others might be called
"poaching." I suppose that wartime gave us a kind of license to
do such things.

MISSION NUMBER 25: APRIL 14, 1945, POINTE DE GRAVE, FRANCE

There was a pocket of German resistance on the west coast of
France. Our target was flak and artillery pieces of large cal-
iber. We were supposed to get moderate flak, but due to surprise and our bombs' exploding around their guns, we received
none. The Germans were causing a lot of trouble to the
French in this area with raids. They were being supplied by
captured allied aircraft and their own submarines. Our job
was strictly a softening-up process. The plan was for the
French to attack after our pasting. We carried a load of four,
2000-pound GP bombs.

Bombing was "super" excellent. In fact, we set the all-time record for the entire 8th Air Force in Europe on this raid. All three squadrons had their bombs entirely in the 1000-foot circle with a high percentage in 500 feet. The entire 8th Air Force hit targets of this kind. Just imagine 27 aircraft, and 27 times 4 equals 108 1-ton bombs all within 1000 feet of the aiming point with nearly 60 percent within 500 feet. One factor contributing to our accuracy was that we bombed from only 15,000 feet and did not have to worry about maneuvering to avoid flak or fighters.

One of our blockbusters hung up in our racks. We had to leave the formation so that we could drop it in the sea. For some time we threaded our way among flak batteries and finally dropped it about 50 miles north of where we bombed. After more threading, we were finally in the clear. But in the process, after being airborne for 9 hours, we ran so short of fuel that we had to land at Manston, England. This was an emergency field with a runway 12,000 feet long and 450 feet wide. A WAAF took us in, and a U.S. captain took our picture (for publicity purposes) around a bottle of Scotch (which didn't

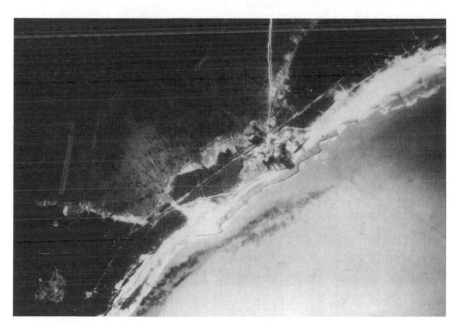

FIGURE 10-1.   The first concentration of bombs at Pointe de Grave, France.

last long). This pretty WAAF then took us to chow and all around the base. The flight time from Manston to Rackheath was 1 hour giving us a total time of 10 hours on this mission.

MISSION NUMBER 26: APRIL 15, 1945, ROYAN, FRANCE

This was just across the channel from the place we bombed the previous day. Our load, a dangerous one to carry, was six 85-gallon napalm fire bombs and two 75-pound bombs of the same stuff. Flight time was 8½ hours. We were to bomb well-entrenched troop concentrations and burn them out so that the French could attack 1 hour later. The fire bombs were

FIGURE 10-2. Total group bomb bursts giving us the all-time 8th Air Force record for bombing accuracy.

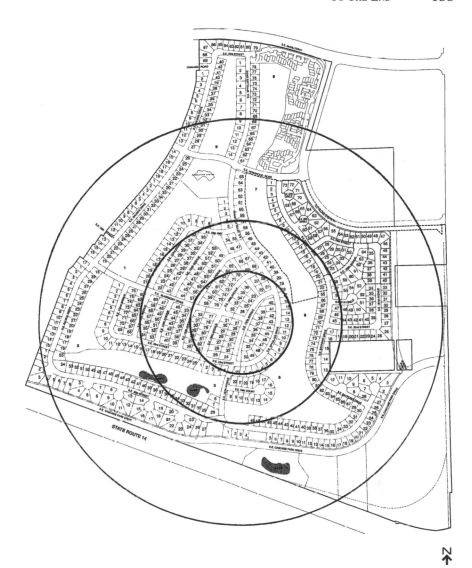

FIGURE 10-3.   Showing 500-, 1000-, and 2000-foot circles superimposed on a map of the author's residential neighborhood. Homes average close to 2000 square feet in area with some adjacent to greens on a 9-hole golf course. Author's lot is number 5 just within the 500-foot circle. A 1-ton bomb packs considerably more power than the bomb that destroyed the government building in Oklahoma.

tumbling as they went down. Two of ours hit just below our plane and burned the rest of the way down. There was a lot of flak in front of us, but our luck still held, and it stopped just as we got to it. Again we bombed from 15,000 feet.

MISSION NUMBER 27: APRIL 16, 1945, LANDSHUT, GERMANY

The bomb load was 11, 500-pound GPs. We bombed the third-priority target by radar because there was a shelf of clouds over the first- and second-priority targets. As it was, the whole route was visual. There were many German aircraft in the area, but none attacked our formation. The marshalling yard was already a shambles from previous raids, but we hit it anyway. On the way in, two of our planes collided. Going out the same thing happened but not in our group. On the way out we were 8 miles left of course and went through the intense flak at Augsburg. A terrific barrage of 88-mm flak was thrown up at us but it was all off of our right wing with a little on our left wing. One of our planes got its left rudder shot off. Since we were leading the wing, the Jerries were just zeroing in on us. The other groups in our wing fared poorly and lost several aircraft. The bombing was good, except that one squadron, because the yard already was wrecked, picked a different MPI and therefore was rated poor. The other squadrons got most of their bombs in the 1000-foot circle. We bombed from 18,000 feet and were at 17,000 feet when hit by flak. Lt. Belingheri had returned from the hospital, and he flew this one with us. But this was his last mission with our crew and, I believe, his last mission with the group.

MISSION NUMBER 28: APRIL 17, 1945, KARLSBAD, CZECHOSLOVAKIA

The bomb load was 10, 500-pound GPs. Time was $7\frac{1}{2}$ hours. We bombed from 17,000 feet. The target was a small marshalling yard in the western part of the country. There were few strategic targets left, so we bombed to help Patton who, characteristically, was not far away. The mission was flown under visual conditions, and the target received a thorough pasting. Except for seeing jets in the area, which did not attack, the mission was uneventful and a milk run. The junction box for the nose gunner's heating suit failed, and so I shared mine with him, alternating from one to the other. I didn't get cold.

MISSION NUMBER 29: APRIL 20, 1945, ZWIESEL, GERMANY

We carried five 1000-pound GPs. Flight duration was 8 hours. The target was a railroad bridge at a small town. The mission was a milk run although fighters were seen in the area. Today marked the best bombing that a single squadron ever did for the 8th Air Force. Out of the first squadron, only three bombs hit outside the 500-foot circle, and these were on the border. Since we were flying wing on the high right, these bombs probably came from our ship. But that was only natural even for the tightest of formations. The other two squadrons got all of their bombs in the 1000-foot circle. Another award-winning feat by our bomb group and by our squadron.

MISSION NUMBER 30: APRIL 21, 1945, SALZBURG, AUSTRIA

The primary target was the marshalling yard. We carried five 1000-pound GPs, and the flying time was 8½ hours. We took off right in the middle of a cold front and had to climb to 10,000 feet in order to get over it on our way to Liege where we formed. It was much too low to go under. Under poor conditions, we formed at Liege starting at 8000 feet but were slowly forced to 4000 feet because of a lowered ceiling. Even so, we were still flying formation through clouds part of the time. When we left, we quickly climbed to 21,000 feet. G was very poor, and we did not see the ground very much. We were flying through clouds occasionally. We got so far off course that we flew right over the center of Regensberg, which was visual at the time. Other groups in our wing lost heavily, and we had two with serious damage. When we reached the group initial point, a huge cloud bank settled in front of us. Unlike the B-17s, we could not go over it, and going under it would have been suicidal. So we decided to turn around and bring our bombs all the way back to our base. Again we went over Regensberg, and again the groups in our wing lost a few ships although we were not touched. We did go under the front on the way back over occupied Germany. The clouds were so low that the lead ship would run through the scud, and we would have to break formation occasionally to get around hills and trees. Finally we had to quit the formation and come home alone. The ceiling was so low that we had to go around church steeples and trees to keep visual. This was a very dangerous flight, and we brought our bombs all the way back and sweat gas. Weather at the base was fairly good. We got credit for the mission because we were shot at.

An almost amusing incident while we were flying near the surface came on the nose gunner's intercom. "Nose gunner to pilot. There's a church steeple ahead." (Silence.) "Nose gunner to pilot. Do you see that steeple just ahead?" (Silence.) "Nose gunner to pilot. Turn, please turn!" Clearly, the pilot was teasing.

Comment: Since the end of the war, and actually only recently, I have come across stories told by crew members in other B-24 bomb groups. Our mission to Salzburg was led by the 466th Bomb Group. They experienced deteriorating weather and drifted off course, heading for Regensburg. The copilot of the plane below and behind the lead, after being advised by his navigator, tried to tell the pilot of the lead plane that they were off course and headed for trouble. But he was told to get off the radio so that a weather report could be heard. Then suddenly the element leader took a direct hit, rolled over, and blew up after falling 500 to 1000 feet. The copilot who voiced the objection performed a violent maneuver in order to avoid debris. Other aircraft in the group sustained considerable damage plus purple hearts. Did the lead navigator screw up? He is too dead to tell. This was just one of several tragedies that resulted from a faulty lead. Our group had considerable damage, but we did not lose any planes.

Another comment: According to a letter published in the *Second Air Division Newsletter*, Salzburg, Austria, was in a different battle zone called the "North Apennines Campaigne." Apparently going on this mission qualifies those in our group who participated for an additional battle star on their campaign ribbons. I don't think any of us realized this at the time, and we never received the extra one. A battle star is supposedly worth an extra 5 "points." I have no idea as to what added benefits this might provide.

MISSION NUMBER 31: APRIL 25, 1945, TRAUNSTEIN, GERMANY

We carried 20, 260-pound fragmentation bombs. Flight time was 8 hours, and we bombed from 21,000 feet. We were briefed for meager flak but got none. The mission was a milk run. Our target was a transformer station attacked by request of the army under General Patton. The weather was visual, and with new G chains navigation was very simple. The target was destroyed.

This was the last mission that the 8th Air Force flew in Europe. The wonderful day of liberation, Victory in Europe Day (VE Day) came on May 8, 1945.

THE LAST FLIGHTS AND THEREAFTER

TROLLEY MISSION

In order to show appreciation to the ground crews who had long fought the European war with dedication and skill in the grooming of the big bombers for flights over heavily defended Germany, the high command invented the Trolley Mission. This was a low-altitude sweep over many important and large German cities so that the passengers could get a good look at the destruction that the heavies (and ground troops) had wrought. The main part of the run consisted of traveling down the Rhine Valley at an altitude not much above the cliffs that border it. No one could understand just how completely this part of Germany had been wasted without actually seeing it. Whole cities that were nothing but piles of rubble without even walls standing. Most cities were completely gutted except for some of the outlying residential districts.

Our crew of five, the skeleton crew composed of pilot, copilot, navigator, radio operator, and engineer, flew with 15 passengers, all ground personnel. While on the trip, I acted as instructor navigator to one of the S2 officers (security) who wanted to be checked out in DR navigation. Something very unusual happened on the trip. Even though it was weeks after VE Day (Victory in Europe), we saw the last of the German flak. It came at us from the Dunkirk pocket only 2 hours before they surrendered. We were about 8 miles to one side of

FIGURE 11-1.   Cathedral at Cologne.

this pocket, but since we were at such a low altitude, the Germans were able to lower their guns and come quite close to our ships, but not too uncomfortably close. It was amusing to watch the expressions on the faces of the ground personnel and hear their words. Why were they shooting at us? Their eyes bugged out at least 3 feet.

In Belgium we flew over the largest prisoner of war camp I have ever seen. There were a half million German prisoners in a large enclosure, all living in pup tents. Men were marching and indulging in calisthenics. Coming back, we went over Holland and saw Rotterdam and The Hague. Since our policy had been to create as little damage as possible in the invaded countries, Holland was hardly touched by the mighty hand of airborne destruction. These cities seemed to be very active and clean. The Dutch grow their vegetables in hothouses. There are huge areas of these structures, all glass.

The trip took 7 hours including the trip across the channel where many rusting hulks could be seen. Needless to say, the ground personnel were very glad to land and some even patted the ground. I think that, between the flak and airsickness, they were getting tired of flying.

FIGURE 11-2.   Part of the city of Bremen.

FIGURE 11-3.   Remagen Bridge days after first crossing.

We flew as a single ship over a common route. Some fool-hardy pilots flew just a few feet above the surface of the Rhine. At least one of these careless pilots could not make it over a bridge with all aboard being killed.

COMING HOME

We flew home in one of our B-24s, complete with guns. Each plane carried 20 men and their baggage. My original pilot was in the hospital and was replaced by Lt. Wallace. My original copilot had been assigned to some different activity, the nature of which I never knew. He was replaced by Lt. Nash. The crew did not include a bombardier. We three officers had a baggage allowance of 65 pounds each. My original crew of noncommissioned personnel was aboard along with 12 members of our ground crew. Enlisted personnel had a baggage allowance of 55 pounds. Clearly, we remained together as an experienced fighting team. The airplane carried 2700 gallons of fuel (topped off) and grossed at 62,000 pounds.

In preparing for the flight, I had to work the hardest. The 8th Air Force crews were not experienced in long, overwater flights, and I studied in order to be sure that I would not "blow it." A lot of people depended on the navigator.

We finally left Rackheath on June 10, 1945. Our first stop was Valley, Wales, which was a major Air Transport Command (ATC) base. The distance was only 275 miles and under 2 hours of flight time, 1 hour of which was actual instruments (AI), or "blind" flying.

On June 11, we left for Meeks Field, Iceland, a distance of about 1000 miles. It took about 6 hours, of which 4 hours

FIGURE 11-4. Bingen-am-Rhine.

FIGURE 11-5.   Scenes from the waist.

FIGURE 11-6.   More scenes.

FIGURE 11-7.   Our picture of Remagen Bridge.

FIGURE 11-8.   Our picture of cathedral at Cologne.

were AI. The route passed over Stoneway, Scotland. My ship was one of the few with Loran. In order to get long-range readings, we put out an antenna, a hundred feet or so long, as a trailing wire beneath the ship. We flew at 8000 feet where the temperature was −5 degrees Celsius. During the AI part of the trip, I could not use the Loran because of "precipitation static" caused by droplets of moisture hitting the antenna. I was able to take some sun shots with the sun being visible through the thin cloud layer above us. The last part of the trip gave us clear weather, and the Loran worked fine. Landing at Meeks in the afternoon was without incident.

Our ships were not heated, and they could be windy. The human mass in the waist was cold and somewhat miserable (a pitiful sight). I had the urge to urinate, which I did on the nose wheel doors. During landing and takeoff, I would be located on the flight deck, taking my nose position only during flight. As a rule, I would crawl past the nose wheel while the doors were closed. Our gradual descent from 8000 feet had warmed things up. As I was almost past the nose wheel on my way to the flight deck, the gear was let down with an unwelcome shower as a result. On subsequent legs of the journey, I decided to use the one and only relief tube. It happened to be in the tail region. Getting to it required climbing over the huddled masses.

We were weathered in at Meeks Field for the better part of a week because of strong head winds of 100 miles per hour and more. We did go to the town of Keflevic once, obviously looking for the equivalent of a pub. It is a neat and clean place but not nearly as large as the principal city of Reykjavic (which we were not able to visit).

On Saturday, June 16, we took off for Goose Bay, Labrador. The distance of about 1500 miles required 9 hours of flying time. Again we flew at 8000 feet with a temperature of −8 degrees Celsius. We got 4 more hours of AI where Loran didn't work and radio was very poor. I used sun shots and Loran when possible with excellent results, coming in zero-zero (on the nose for both track and time of arrival) at Goose Bay. As we neared Labrador, large ice floes and icebergs could be seen.

We left Goose Bay on June 17 for Bradley Field, Connecticut, a distance of about 1000 miles and a flight time of 6½ hours. I used radio and pilotage (and, as always, DR). Two hours were AI. The flight at 10,000 feet had a temperature ranging from −7 at the start to +11 degrees Celsius at the end. We landed at noon at Bradley after turning back our watches by 4 hours.

After a speedy processing at Bradley, we left by train on June 18 for Camp Miles Standish, Massachusetts, where we did absolutely nothing for two nights. Then individuals went in different directions. I went by slow train for Camp Beal at Marysville, California, to receive a 1-month leave for RRR (rest, recuperation, and rehabilitation). On this part of the trip, I had a 5-hour layover in St. Louis, which was thoroughly enjoyed. The trip from Camp Beale to home was by civilian means (i.e., train) on June 25, 1945. "HOME ALIVE IN FORTY FIVE."

But this was not quite the end of my army career. The Japanese had not yet seen fit to throw in the towel. After my 1-month leave, I reported to a redistribution center in Sioux Falls, South Dakota. The war in the Pacific had not yet ended. From there I was assigned to the ATC stationed in Memphis, Tennessee. The only flying done there was on two search missions, looking for planes reported missing in the general area. This time, aircraft were C-47s (the same as the venerable DC-3). I must admit that a fine time was had in Memphis with local belles.

I had not been in the ATC for long before the "bomb" ended hostilities in the Pacific. Japan surrendered on August 14, 1945. It was not long thereafter that military "downsizing" took place. In November, 1945, I received my orders to report to the San Bernardino Army Air Base and received a certificate of service. A short trip of 40 miles took me back to Pasadena.

THE BOMB

It took quite a while to appreciate the significance of the atom bomb and the destruction of Hiroshima and Nagasaki. Had it not been for this, I suspect that the Japanese would have held on in the hopes of a negotiated settlement, which would have maintained most of their leaders in place, especially the near-god king. Our reluctance to get anything less than an unconditional surrender would have required massive destructive bombing involving not only B-29s but also our B-24s. And, most likely, me. B-17s might also have been used, but these had less range and bomb-carrying capacity than we did. We B-24 crew members would have paid dearly for our attacks.

Information that has only recently come to me states that the 467th was to be converted to handle B-29s. You can certainly get killed in one of these, but perhaps not as quickly as in a B-24.

Recall our invasion of Okinawa. This battle cost thousands of American lives and tens of thousands of Japanese civilian casualties. Projecting this sort of scenario to Japan would likely have resulted in many hundreds of thousands of Japanese fatalities and tens of thousands of American lives in an invasion. Germany did not surrender and remained defiant clear up to the walls of Hitler's personal bunker. There is reason to think that Japanese leaders would have made similar sacrifices; for they had already indicated their willingness to act as human bombs with the Kamikazi aircraft attacks.

The bomb answered all of these "what-if" questions. Its existence suggests that the bloody Okinawa invasion, late in the war, was really not necessary. Those killed in nuclear explosions were few in number compared to what a conventional onslaught would have achieved. Lives saved could very well have included my own!

What resulted from total capitulation of both Germany and Japan? These countries are now free and have become major players in the world's economy. In some respects, they have fared better than our allies!

Would a single nonlethal demonstration of the power of the bomb have caused the Japanese to give up? I think not. They would have assumed that the demonstration was a magic trick or a Hollywood production.

Our development and use of the bomb did start another "war," namely, the "cold war" between Russia and us. Paranoia resulted in our tendency toward a police state where liberal thoughts were viewed as seditious. But this too passed. Had the world not actually witnessed the awesome destructive power of the bomb, I suspect that our adversary would not have considered it to be as destructive as it was. They (Russia) might have chanced an outright attack, which would have imperiled our very civilization.

We have the continuing fear that some desperate group or third-world nation might use the bomb against us, possibly blaming some outlaw group for the act. What could we possibly do if we knew that some group was prepared to explode a bomb hidden somewhere in Washington, D.C.? It is naive to think that, had we not developed the thing, its secrets would have remained as such. Without the bomb, would the earth's family of major nations have cooperated to the extent that we see today?

I rank the bomb and the discovery of how to (more or less) harness nuclear energy as one of the great achievements in human history. So as to not seem biased, I will add what I consider to be two other great moments: the Apollo 12 and the first presence of human beings on the moon and the discovery of the double helix.

READJUSTING

Aging vets tend to look back on their wartime experience as being one of the most influential and unforgettable parts of their lives. Even those who did not experience combat are similarly influenced. Sending a young person away for a time, into an unfamiliar environment, and then dumping him or her back into the environment from whence he or she came can indeed be traumatic. The year or two that a youth develops into adulthood must leave lasting impressions no matter what the environment.

Giving someone who is barely emerging from the teenage years the importance and influence of an officer may or may not be a justifiable act. But it does pose a risk of adding to the difficulty of readjusting upon return to the preservice environment.

Had it not been for an intense motivation for higher education, I might have had more problems than I did.

I do recall two incidents of a meaningful kind. A long leave for RRR included the Fourth of July celebration of 1945 at the Pasadena Rose Bowl. The explosions got to me. I almost "freaked out" and had to be calmed and reassured by my parents. A second incident can be blamed on a wishful desire to relive the bawdy brotherhood of airmen in England. I was picked up, almost passed out in a drunken stupor, next to my car in downtown Los Angeles. In those days, being alone at night in such a place was nowhere near as dangerous as it is today. The police took me, and I spent the night in the drunk tank. Breakfast was "gruel" of some kind without milk or sugar. My father bailed me out that morning. The car was not impounded. No one chastised me for my behavior, police or parents. I think it was generally understood that lots of us were having emotional problems.

Although we did booze a lot in the service, I was fortunate in not developing an alcoholic's cravings for the stuff. After the war I never drank at all during the week because it interfered too much with studies. Party time was another matter, but not to an excess leading to loss of control.

A BRIEF POSTWAR HISTORY

The return to full civilian status was in November, 1945. I returned to studies at Pasadena Junior College as soon as possible (February, 1946), receiving the AA degree in the summer of 1946 (after carrying a quite heavy load). Upon graduation I was honored with the American Legion Student Award for that year. But 1946 was also a very sad time for me and my parents. My younger brother died of Hodgkin's disease at the age of only 17. He had been a most popular and well-liked person at McKinley Junior High School where he had been captain of the football team and also the student body president. I was the nerd of the family. He was the diplomat and politician. Had we had the medical tools of today back in 1946, he might have lived.

We were surely grief stricken. My reactions were not quite the same as others. I had learned to live with death on an almost daily basis. One must compartmentalize the mind so that concerns for friends are forgotten in order to do the job at hand. One does not really forget. But sadness can be made to come less frequently through "death training." I don't know if I was viewed by others as being hard or unconcerned. I certainly was not. In this case, the job at hand was education.

In the fall of 1946, I transferred as a junior to Stanford University. We lived in a conventional army barracks with 20 or so beds and toilet and showers at one end. The place was called "Stanford Village." At least we didn't have drill sergeants to harass us! At that time, the tuition at Stanford was only $120 per quarter. The GI bill was sufficient to pay this along with lodging, books, and food. It took a bit extra for carousing.

After being there a short time, a second tragedy befell our family. My father died suddenly of a massive heart attack. He was only 51. He smoked (a lot) and was overweight. I left Stanford and returned to Pasadena in order to help clear things up and aid my mother who was now all alone. But I did plan on returning to Stanford, and so I was tutored (in circuit analysis) by a student at Cal Tech. This was the one subject area that would be hard to replace without significant educational delay.

We sold the home, and I moved with my mother to a new small house in Menlo Park, California, which is contiguous with Stanford University. She secured a teaching position at a prestigious girls' school in Menlo Park. As I recall, the cost of the house was appreciably under $10,000. I continued my education, receiving the B.S. in electrical engineering in 1948 and the M.S. in 1949.

The next place was Pasadena, California, and a job at Cal Tech's Jet Propulsion Lab. What I did there has previously been highlighted. The salary was quite good at $350 per month. The going rate today for a person with the degrees would be over $4500 per month. But $350 went a lot further than it does today. My rather nice apartment cost $65 per month. A good late-model used car went for only a few hundred dollars. Everything was much less costly in terms of dollars. The difference is not as great if dollars are

converted to present equivalent amounts. The main excep-
tions are medical care and college tuition, which have both
risen considerably more than most other costs. For example,
a month's salary of $350 would pay tuition for almost a
whole academic year at Stanford.

My time at Stanford corresponded to a period when the veteran student population was large. We all worked very hard,
which no doubt put a lot of pressure on nonveterans because
grading was "on the curve." After the veteran student bulge had
passed, test grades in the classes that had previously been most
populated by veterans dropped 15 or 20 percent.

Leland Stanford created his university with the objective
of making it affordable to all. This it was until destructive
inflationary pressures began to be felt in the late 1950s and
1960s. The cost of a higher education beyond that provided
at community colleges has risen to the point where, without a
scholarship, only the well-to-do can afford it without mort-
gaging the home. When I was there, many nonveterans were
able to work their way through, living off campus in rooming
houses or in rented rooms. I suspect that statistics will show
that an increasing number of families with lower-than-average
incomes are no longer able to send their children through
four years of college, much less to graduate school.

But back to a brief history, at least to the point where I met
and married Rita. In the spring of 1951, I left the Jet
Propulsion Lab and went to work for Hughes Aircraft Company
in Culver City, California. Howard Hughes himself would occasionally roam the corridors at night, turning off unneeded
lights. My job was mathematical analysis trying to improve the
ability of radar to detect a moving object close to the ground.
The system was the Air Moving Target Indicator, or AMTI for
short. This is a very tough problem. Two of us, a Ph.D. and
myself, were able to apply second-order statistics to give a pretty
fair theoretical model.

During this period, I met Rita. Her uncle had sponsored
her from England in order to further her education. What
she got in England was spotty and incomplete because of
frequent bombings, rockets, and evacuations to the countryside. She didn't get too much chance for further education

because I intervened. We were married on September 15, 1951, with a civil ceremony at my mother's apartment. We then immediately left for Stanford for further graduate work. Tuition had risen from $120 per quarter to $220. Our abode was first a room in a boarding house with one bathroom at the end of the hall. Soon after we moved back to Stanford Village. But this time it was in a barracks that was divided into several small apartments. It was a good time. I worked very hard and finally received the doctorate in 1953. From there, a job as assistant professor of electrical engineering awaited me at the University of Michigan. It was there, in Ann Arbor, that our two sons were born.

And that's enough of a personal history except for one more thing. I have a card that shows I was in the Acting Air Force Reserve for 1 day in 1952. The Korean conflict waged. Navigators, especially seasoned ones, were in short supply. They would be put in twin-engine attack bombers where life expectancy was shorter than it had been in the 8th Air Force. I was ordered to Oakland for an interview and physical. At the time I had the flu with a temperature of 102 degrees. But orders are orders, and so I went. The examining physician did a truly great favor for me that saved my educational career, possibly a brand-new marriage, and maybe even my life. He decided that I had evidence of rails from asthma and disqualified me to the "honorary" reserve.

THE B-24 AND STATISTICS

INTRODUCTION

There remain some "loose ends" to my story that need to be covered. First, I will say something about the venerable B-24 and how it can be compared to the other principal American heavy bomber, the B-17. Comments on overall losses in the air war will then be discussed. Finally, a discussion of wing theory is presented including characteristics of lift, drag, and aspect ratio. It was not unusual to relate the B-24's most important feature to its use of the "Davis wing" (which was later adopted for the B-29).

THE B-24 IN COMBAT

The air war in Europe involved many aircraft created by British and American designers (plus the Germans, of course). In addition to the heavies, we had twin-engine bombers (B-25, B-26, and A-26) and fighters (P-38, P-47, and P-51). The British had four engine bombers that flew mostly at night. They also had Spitfire and Hawker Hurricane fighters. Their popular, light, two-engine bomber was the Mosquito.

The heavies that operated out of Africa and Italy were mostly B-24s. These were outnumbered in England by the B-17s, two divisions to our one. In the Pacific theater, we used B-24s and the navy version, which was like the B-24 except that it had a single tall tail and some features of comfort such as waist windows that could be closed. The B-29s came along later in the war. Considering all theaters of war, the B-24 had a significantly greater role than did the B-17. For some reason, however, the B-17 seems to have received all of the glory. There is one exception, namely, the B-24s involved in early raids on German oil facilities at Ploesti, Romania. On that first mission, 177 started, 53 were shot down, and another 55 managed to return with damage so extensive that many were simply salvaged.

One B-24 group in the 8th Air Force is "credited" with the greatest loss on a single mission of any group in the 8th Air Force. It was September, 1944, to Kassel, Germany. Even worse, the raid failed to achieve its objective. Of 35 planes that started, only 5 survived. Few have heard of this.

The B-17 was an operational bomber before the B-24. It was our primary bomber during the first part of our involvement in Europe until approximately the middle of 1943 when B-24s began to arrive. (Few B-17s were involved in the African or Italian campaigns.) Stories abound of crews barely making it back in B-17s that looked like Swiss cheese. Our B-24s did not glide as well as the B-17s, and to ditch one in the ocean could prove fatal. The high wing made crash landings more dangerous. Both B-17s and B-24s operating out of England needed to clear only the cliffs of Dover or pass the coastline in order to get home. B-24s out of Italy had to cross the Alps, which was impossible without adequate power. The net result was that damaged B-24s were less likely to return to their bases than were the B-17s, and hence fewer tall tales could be told. It is estimated that for every three B-17 crew members that were killed, five were lost in B-24s.

The Davis wing of the B-24 was a high-performance wing with an appearance not unlike that of a soaring glider—long, thin, and narrow. Its advantage was a greater lift-to-drag ratio than more conventional airfoils. A somewhat "war-weary" photograph of our plane in flight is shown in Figure 12-1. With the Davis wing, the B-24 was able to fly further with a larger bomb load than the B-17. And faster as well. However, it would not get to as high an altitude with a comparable bomb load, which made the B-24 more susceptible to flak. But this gave the B-24 an advantage in achieving better bombing accuracy. The Davis wing turned out to be preferred for piston bomber aircraft and was redesigned and reconfigured for the B-29.

The B-17 used the single-row Wright Cyclone engine. We had the double-row Pratt Whitney, which was considered by many to be more reliable and more efficient.

B-24 SPECIFICATIONS

Span	110 feet
Length	66 feet, 4 inches
Height	17 feet, 11 inches
Weight	56,000 pounds, loaded
Armament	10, 0.50-caliber machine guns and 8000 pounds of bombs
Engines	Four Pratt Whitney R-1830s of 1200 horsepower each
Crew	10
Cost	$336,000 (1944 dollars)
Maximum speed	303 miles per hour
Cruise speed	175 miles per hour
Range	3200 miles
Service ceiling	28,000 feet

The above specifications err in some respects. With full fuel of 2700 gallons (topped off) and a full bomb load, we grossed 72,000 pounds. At least during the English winter, this weight posed little problem. The air was cold, and the field elevation was only a couple of hundred feet above sea level. The density altitude was thus low and generally favored getting maximum power at takeoff. The specifications of speed and range are not related to any particular altitude. The implied altitude is probably around 8000 feet, which favors

FIGURE 12-1.   Author's B-24 in flight showing long wings.

maximum range in terms of speed relative to the rate of fuel
consumption. When at high altitude with superchargers, the
fuel burn rate was relatively high. We rarely could get much
more than 9 hours out of 2700 gallons of fuel, which suggests
an average rate of consumption approaching 300 gallons per
hour. The numbers given in the specifications imply a maximum duration of over 18 hours and hence a fuel burn rate of
approximately 150 gallons per hour. (Divide the specified
range by the specified cruise speed in order to get the duration
of flight, with values in statute, rather than nautical, miles.)
This favored the use of B-24s in the Pacific theater for long
overwater flights at medium altitudes.

The airspeed given in the specifications is about correct if
it is specified in statute miles per hour and applies to
midrange altitudes. In terms of nautical miles, the value at
around 8000 feet drops to the range 155 to 165 knots. At high
altitudes, the true airspeed was in the range 180 to 190 knots.

The specifications do not apply to our bombers for another
reason. We carried 8 machine guns instead of 10. This was
because we had removed the ball turret.

When flying at high altitude with a full bomb load, the orientation of the aircraft clearly showed that the angle of attack of the wing was appreciably greater than at lower altitudes. Furthermore, the wing with load showed a distinct upward curvature, and the thing would wobble up and down when turbulence was present.

LOSSES AND STATISTICS

In 1944 alone, flak destroyed 3501 American bombers, and German fighters destroyed about 2900 more. These numbers might surprise some because popular lore considered German fighters to be more dangerous than antiaircraft fire. For the several years of air combat in Europe, we lost almost 10,000 bombers (of all types) plus another 8000 that were damaged beyond repair. The Army Air Force as a whole suffered more than 120,000 battle casualties (dead, wounded, and missing), and almost all were flying personnel.

All told, more than 19,000 B-24 bombers were built, mostly for the air force but also about 1700 for the navy. Over 50,000 B-24 airmen (not including the B-17) were killed, injured, or became prisoners of war. In the Second Air Division in England, 7000 were killed outright, and thousands more were wounded and/or held as prisoners of war in Germany.

The Second Air Division consisted of 14 bomb groups and 5 fighter groups. Each group had several squadrons, almost all of which operated in daylight bombing missions. The Second Air Division had a total of about 1500 B-24s with perhaps a third of these participating in a typical mission. Another 1000 B-24s were in the 15th Air Force operating out of Italy.

Even though the United States sustained grievous loss of life (all branches of the military), it was nothing compared to what the Russians or the Germans lost. For the USSR, the peak strength of the military was over 12 million with well over 6 million battle deaths. Compare this to the United States with a comparable peak strength but less than 300,000 battle deaths. The axis powers lost heavily as well with Germany/Austria

having about 4 million killed out of a peak strength of
10 million. In Japan the numbers were around 1.6 million
and 6 million. The USSR seems to win this "contest" with
Germany close behind.

WING THEORY

The plan view of a wing is what you see looking down from
above. Wingspan tip to tip includes the width of the fuselage,
which does not contribute to lift and should not be considered
to be part of the wing area. Wing calculations and wind tunnel
tests ignore the fuselage (albeit, wind tunnel tests can use
complete models as well as wing models alone). Wing area is
an important number. The aspect ratio is another important
one. What is *aspect ratio*? For a simple rectangular wing, it is
the length from tip to tip (not including the fuselage) divided
by the width. For shapes other than the rectangle, it is the
square of the length divided by the area. The aspect ratio of the
B-24 wing (both halves) is 11.2. (That for the B-17 is 7.68.)
The total wing area is approximately 750 square feet, although
allowances must be made for engines. The plan view of the
wing of the B-24 (one side) is shown in Figure 12-2.

The cross section of a wing is called the *airfoil section*. An
example is shown in Figure 12-3. This particular shape is cat-
aloged as NACA 4415. The letters stand for National Advisory
Committee for Aeronautics. After the war, this organization

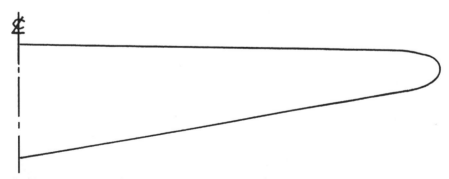

FIGURE 12-2.   Plan view of one-half of the Davis wing.

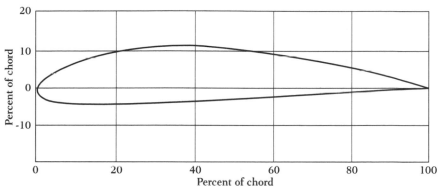

FIGURE 12-3. Cross section of NACA 4415 wing.

was changed to NASA, which stands for National Aeronautics and Space Administration. It may surprise some to know that this wing section was tested way back in 1931.

The *chord* of the airfoil section is measured from the forward part of the front edge of the wing to the rear tip. The chord line is shown for the section of Figure 12-3 (the zero line). In flight, the wing is tilted slightly upward in order to generate sufficient lift. The angle of the chord line with respect to the horizontal path of the wing in air is called the *angle of attack*.

Air moving over the top surface of a wing when the angle of attack is greater than a small negative value has a longer path to travel from nose to tip than does the air on the bottom surface. The air molecules on the top then have a reduced tendency to strike the wing surface perpendicular to it, thus giving a lower pressure than on the bottom surface. (The air inside the wing is neutral with the same pressure applied to the inner surfaces of both top and bottom skins.) Toward the end of the wing, air can move laterally from higher to lower pressure regions, which reduces total lift. A short stubby wing (low aspect ratio) is less efficient than one with a large aspect ratio because the end effect is more pronounced. However, when the wing is oriented to provide only a small lift, the difference in pressure between top and bottom surfaces is so small that little air moves laterally. For small lift, this results in wings of relatively low aspect ratios performing almost as well as those with high ratios. An aspect ratio above 10 or 15 gives efficiency within a few percent of the maximum that is possible, which applies to a wing with *infinite aspect ratio*.

A short rectangular wing can be made with a uniform airfoil section and confined between parallel plates so that end effects are avoided. Such a section can be tested in a wind tunnel. The principal measures one gets are the lift, the drag, and the moment. Surfaces of the test section are made as smooth as possible (like glass) in order to get measures as close to the induced drag component as possible. Measured values when converted to apply to a unit wing length are called *coefficients of lift and drag*. The *moment* is important because it tells if changes in lift will tend to lower or raise the nose of the airplane (because the center of pressure can change with angle of attack).

Tests as described are labeled *section tests*. They are not the same as tests of a complete wing including its (usually) rounded tips. A wind tunnel can test either sections or complete wings (or complete model airplanes for that matter). Wing theory allows the performance of complete wings to be calculated from section test data. The nature of a section test with a short section between relatively large end plates (to prevent lateral air movements) gives the result of a hypothetical wing of infinite aspect ratio.

Coefficients of lift and drag depend upon the angle of attack. For an unsymmetric airfoil section as in Figure 12-3, some positive lift can occur at a zero or even a small negative angle of attack. For a symmetrical shape, zero lift corresponds to an angle of attack of zero. In either case, the lift curve is remarkably straight up to near its peak when it levels off and falls more or less rapidly. The solid lines in Figure 12-4 are curves for the coefficients of lift, drag, and moment for the Davis wing, where that for drag is expressed in terms of the coefficient of lift rather than the angle of attack.

Important note: A complete model for the Davis wing is represented by the test results shown in Figure 12-4—not a section.

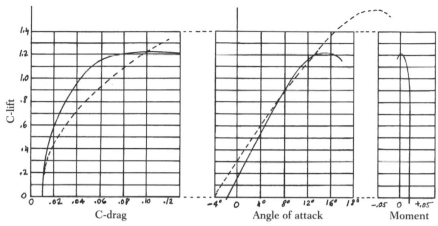

FIGURE 12-4. Lift and drag for the Davis wing (solid lines) and NACA 4415 (dashed lines).

The coefficient of drag tends to be flat and relatively small at coefficients of lift that are most likely to be used. Drag increases at an increasing rate as the lift (or angle of attack) increases. For some airfoil sections, not described here, the drag curve has a more or less narrow and well-defined "bucket" in the central part, which is called the *drag bucket*.

Drag of the wing has two components. One is called *induced drag*, which can be measured along with minimum *skin friction*. No surface has ever been produced that avoids a minimum amount of skin friction. The minimum value for drag shown in Figure 12-4 is that due to skin friction; the Davis test wing surface was as smooth as glass. If the wing is not perfectly smooth, there will be additional parasitic drag. A *standard roughness model* is often specified in section curves. The result of this roughness is a total drag that is about twice the sum of induced drag and skin friction and tends to suppress the presence of a drag bucket (if any).

What is *induced drag*? The airplane stays at a constant altitude by riding on a cushion of air. The air, being compressible, moves downward. The process is one of action and reaction. Like a fan blade or a propeller, there is a *downwash*. Bending the airstream downward requires energy to keep the wing moving at a constant velocity while carrying a load, which equates to drag. Drag must be overcome with engine power.

The ratio of lift to drag as a function of the angle of attack reveals the point where efficiency is a maximum. This ratio can be computed from the curve of lift versus drag. For the NACA 4415 the peak ratio is about 20. For the Davis wing it is approximately 30.

Induced drag is only one component of total drag. In wind tunnel tests, very smooth test wing surfaces are used so as to get as close to the perfect wing as possible. A second measurement of drag is made when the wing surface is given a standard roughness. This does not appreciably affect the lift curve, but it will raise the drag curve by a factor of 2 or more and may eliminate the drag bucket (if any). Any irregularities on the wing, including rivets, bugs, etc., will cause some small amount of turbulence to be created, and the sum of all of these small events increases drag by a substantial amount.

What is the nature of skin friction? Air moving over a flat plate parallel to its surface has some frictional effects when air molecules strike the surface in such a way that their individual velocities are reduced (on average), perhaps because they hit a projection of molecular size. This skin friction sets a minimum to the drag curve. Even in the absence of skin irregularities, there will always be some skin friction due to the slowing effect of molecules as they scrape along the surface. This minimum drag case is called *laminar flow*. With visible surface irregularities, air immediately adjacent to the surface experiences *turbulent flow*. The thin film of air near the surface is referred to as the *boundary layer*, which can contain either laminar or turbulent flow. The drag in this latter case can be twice that given for laminar flow, increasing to 10 times as much or more at high Reynolds numbers. Very high velocity aircraft, missiles, and space vehicles returning to earth experience such high skin friction that the surfaces can heat to dangerous levels. Refractory materials are placed on the skin surfaces of returning space shuttles for this reason.

What is the *Reynolds number*? It is a measure that relates to compressibility and viscosity of air. It tends to measure the tendency of an airflow to become turbulent. A simplified alternate definition is a number applied to flight at a constant altitude (air pressure) that is proportional to the product of velocity and width of the wing. A high velocity and small width can give the same Reynolds number as a wide wing at a low speed. The Reynolds number is also proportional to air density and thus decreases as altitude increases. (The density of air molecules decreases with altitude such that fewer such molecules collide with the surface of the wing at high altitudes.) In wind tunnel tests using small models, the tunnel is pressurized so that the Reynolds number can be similar to that of a full-size model. Surprisingly, the Reynolds number does not affect lift and drag of a wing very much until it gets so large as to suggest velocities beginning to approach the speed of sound.

There are other components of drag that include the fuselage with various projections, engines and the ram air needed for cooling, and the tail surface. The horizontal tail, which also contributes to drag, will normally be oriented so that it has a small negative lift, just the reverse of what the wing provides. For a very *dirty* airplane (i.e., lots of drag in addition to the induced drag), the advantage of a high-efficiency wing as opposed to a low-efficiency one having adequate lift may be small. In such cases, total wingspan with a relatively small aspect ratio may influence design. A high lift wing with high induced drag may be quite satisfactory and in some cases preferred (such as for crop dusting).

What are actual total values of lift and drag? At a given angle of attack, total lift is proportional to wing area, the square of the speed, and the lift coefficient. Drag is calculated exactly the same way except that the total drag coefficient is employed. The same constant of proportionality applies to both lift and drag formulas and is equal to one-half the air density. As the airplane climbs, air density decreases (to about one-half the sea level value at 18,000 feet and one-fifth at 32,000 feet). In order to maintain constant lift, the angle of attack must be increased. Total drag may or may not increase by much depending on whether wing drag or that from other causes dominates. The service ceiling is the altitude where an

increase in angle of attack cannot increase lift enough to overcome reduced air density and increased drag without adding
more engine power. At this point, the airplane is tilted well
upward and is "mushing" along.

A study of airfoil sections applies not only to wings but
also to propellers, fan blades, and helicopter rotors. The hobby
of model airplane building can take advantage of airfoil data
with results similar to what can occur with full-size airplanes.

THE DAVIS WING

The inventor, David Davis, was not an aeronautical engineer. He came up with his design using high school–level
mathematics. He applied for a patent in 1931, which was
issued in 1934 (before actual experimental data were available). He worked with the Consolidated Company in order
to get a model tested at the Guggenheim Aeronautical
Laboratory of California Institute of Technology (GALCIT).
A model of the complete wing was tested in 1937. The story
is that Cal Tech was so slow in returning data that Mr.
Davis called twice to ask why. The reason turned out to be
that performance was so good that the wind tunnel opera-
tors thought they had a problem with instrumentation.

The story of the testing is not only interesting, but it has
considerable historic importance. The original test report, prepared by Dr. Clark Millikan and his staff, is dated September
13, 1937. A true scale model of the wing was tested. It had a
span (both halves) of 90 inches. I will quote some material
directly from this report:

> Certain of the results for the Davis wing are so striking that
> when they were first obtained, it was felt that some experimen-
> tal error must have entered. Accordingly, the model was
> installed in the tunnel and tested on three separate occasions
> some weeks apart. The final Run was made immediately follow-
> ing that with the Consolidated wing. All three tests gave perfect
> agreement. The first and last are plotted together in Fig. 7
> [see our Figure 12-4] and it is seen that the results are indistin-

guishable. The intermediate Run (not plotted) gave exactly the same lift and drag results as those shown here, and the moment curve was also identical except for a very small shift of the curve along the moment axis probably caused by a slight error in setting the zero point of the moment balance. In view of these repeated checks the Davis wing results are believed to be very trustworthy. The comparison between it and the Consolidated wing should be especially good because of the extreme precautions which were taken to make all of the conditions of test as nearly identical as possible for the two cases.

The wind tunnel at GALCIT had an inner dimension of 10 feet. Wings were tested in model form with air density modified so that a small model yielded performance that directly indicated how a full-size wing would perform. Many little corrections to data are needed to account for the effects of supporting structures, instrumentation, and so on. The tested wing was not a section. It was a faithful model with the plan shape of Figure 12-2.

The Davis wing is comparatively thin with a thickness of about 17 percent of the chord near the fuselage falling to under 14 percent near the tip. Thin wings can be more efficient than thicker ones but also can have drag that rises more rapidly with angle of attack. The Davis wing is not sensitive to angle of attack.

Another problem with a thin wing is that it won't contain a strong main wing spar unless the spar is widened at the cost of greater weight than that required for a strong spar in a thicker wing. The extreme practical case of the high-efficiency wing is seen in soaring gliders. These gliders are very light in weight, which minimizes bending stress on the thin wing. But such gliders still are not very safe in turbulence.

The Davis wing was important because it came close to the performance of an ideal (mathematical) thin wing in an ideal fluid. But it was not too thin to hold a good wing spar or to suffer excessive positional sensitivity.

How good is the Davis wing relative to other configurations? A comparison with data in books describing lift and drag properties of various wings is not a direct process. This is because data are for the most part related either to section characteristics (i.e., infinite aspect ratio) or to various wing shapes for a fixed nominal aspect ratio of (typically) 6. The dashed lines in Figure 12-4 apply to a wing with a cross section bearing the NACA 4415 number. The airfoil section is shown in Figure 12-3. The low aspect ratio of 6 shows the drag to be considerably higher for lift coefficients above 0.2 than for the Davis wing. The lift curve as a function of angle of attack is not as steep as that for the Davis wing, although it rises to a higher peak value. *Note:* Lift near the peak value does not represent a practical region of operation because of the large amount of induced drag (albeit, this may not be important if parasitic drag is large by comparison). Correcting the 4415 drag curve to an aspect ration of 11 (similar to the Davis wing) will reduce the drag but not to as low a value as applies to the Davis wing.

Remember the old biplanes of World War I and later, the barnstormers? They had so much parasitic drag that there was little incentive to invent efficient wing section shapes.

One final vignette to this discussion of the Davis wing: Mr. Davis, on his own, made aerodynamic tests in an ersatz "wind tunnel." He borrowed a convertible automobile from a friend. He and a coconspirator would mount a structure on top with a short airfoil section of the wing mounted vertically. Forces equivalent to lift and drag for various angles of attack were obtained while driving down the highway at respectable speeds. The time available for each testing session was limited because the convertible had to be returned to its owner.

DEAD RECKONING

INTRODUCTION

The story presented in the several chapters of this book did not delve into details as to how we navigators made our calculations so as to follow or direct our airplanes through preplanned routes. In this appendix I introduce the reader to the all-important dead-reckoning procedure along with the instruments and devices we routinely employed. At the end I will comment on how the art has changed and how the dedicated navigator has become a dinosaur. Nevertheless, the basic dead-reckoning procedure remains essential to this day and probably will remain so into the distant future. There are changes, however. More computer aids are now in use along with a variety of instruments that provide precise location data.

The bible of the navigator during World War II was the "Navigators' Information File" (NIF). I have borrowed from NIF for drawings and pictures and some direct quotations.

Before proceeding, however, let me describe some postwar experiences. These have served to keep me generally informed about flying and the instruments that are employed. During the period 1960 through 1962, I taught at the University of Arizona in Tucson. While there, I took flying lessons and earned a private pilot's license. A general desire to upgrade led to the commercial license, then ratings for instrument flying and gliding. I also took a course on mountain flying and even tried hang gliding. Until recent years, I was a fairly active flyer in a variety of single-engine aircraft from the Piper Cub to the Bonanza and amateur-built aircraft, with a total time as pilot in command of about 1200 hours. During this period, a gradual improvement in communications and navigating apparatus was followed. The pace of sophistication has quickened, and now the "ultimate" navigational tool has come into the market, namely, the satellite navigation system, referred to as the *ground position system* (GPS). The last section of this appendix discusses some apparatus history and what the future holds.

The Davis-Monthan Air Force Base is located in Tucson. Old warbirds were brought there and scrapped, first those from World War II, then jets from later wars and exercises. The commanding officer when I was in Tucson was the same Col. Shower that we knew. I chatted with him briefly on the telephone, but only that.

DEFINITIONS

I start this section with material drawn from NIF.

> Dead reckoning, the basis of all navigation, is the use of information such as time, speed, and distance from a known position to find unknown data involving the same factors.
>
> 1. In basic dead reckoning, use groundspeed and track-made-good, established directly from two or more known positions.
>
> 2. In precision dead reckoning, use known position, true heading, true airspeed, and wind speed and direction. In ground plot, find the position of your airplane by plotting track-made-good (true heading and wind effect) and groundspeed (true airspeed with wind effect). In air plot, find the no-wind position of your airplane by plotting true heading and true airspeed.
>
> 3. In follow-the-pilot, continuously determine your position, using precision dead reckoning, without controlling the heading or airspeed of the airplane.
>
> A fix is the airplane's position determined by one or more navigational aids.

1. In fix-to-fix procedure, treat single fixes as actual positions.
2. In average track procedure, establish average track and groundspeed by interpreting a series of fixes.

The successful termination of any flight depends on dead reckoning. Navigators returning from all over the world—from the Aleutians, where weather is always a problem; from the Marianas, where long over-water flights are made constantly; from China, the land of no maps—stress this fact: Dead reckoning is the basis of all navigation. Use it. Celestial, pilotage, radio, and Loran all are aids to dead reckoning. Use them only as aids.

Dead reckoning is based upon the solution of the time-speed-distance problem, and you are primarily a dead-reckoning navigator. Pilots dead reckon on every flight, though they are not always aware of this fact. Your work must be more exact, of course, than a pilot's mental calculations. And you must know and use every form of dead reckoning available to you on every flight you make.

If you make but one resolve as a navigator, it should be, "I'll dead reckon on every flight from the time we take off until the wheels are back on the ground." If you do less than this you are not doing your job—and that can easily prove fatal.

To do accurate work, you must be able to recognize all possible errors in your computations and know how to compensate for them. Furthermore, you must understand the navigation problems you are likely to encounter and plan your solutions of them before you leave the ground. Constant air practice then gives you needed confidence.

Prepare adequately on the ground to make your work as easy as possible in the air. The distractions of flight conditions such as combat, weather, and lack of oxygen, and the inconveniences of fatigue and cramped quarters unavoidably complicate your job. Don't make it more difficult for yourself.

VECTORS AND THE WIND TRIANGLE

If you find the following discussion to contain unfamiliar and perhaps confusing concepts, try first reading the last section of this appendix, "A Little Algebra."

The principal arithmetic formula is time and distance. If the aircraft travels at a rate of 180 knots for 1 hour, the distance covered is 180 nautical miles. If travel is for 10 minutes, the distance is one-sixth of 180 because 10 minutes is one-sixth of an hour. In general, formulas are:

Distance = velocity * time
Time = distance/velocity
Velocity = distance/time

where * stands for multiplication and / denotes division.

We generally used nautical miles and nautical miles per hour (knots) in our navigation. A nautical mile is 6080.27 feet. A statute mile is 5280 feet. Dividing one by the other we find that 1 nautical mile equals 1.15166 statute miles. Recall that the nautical mile is 1 minute of arc along a line of constant longitude (a meridian). With 90 degrees from equator to pole and 60 minutes of arc per degree, we find that the distance from equator to pole is 90 * 60 = 5400 nautical miles.

Vectors represent the motion of the airplane with respect to the air mass in which it travels. Here is an example. Assume true airspeed is 180 knots. In 20 minutes, traveling due east, the plane covers 60 (nautical) miles. Then the plane turns to a true north heading and travels for another 40 minutes. Where is it? Figure A-1 shows the vector plot for this situation. The location of the plane is the same as if it had flown along the diagonal. Had it done this, the total distance traveled would have been 134.16 miles instead of 180, and the total time of flight would have been 50 minutes instead of 1 hour.

A problem arises if wind is not zero. If a constant wind of 50 knots from the left (west) was present, and if the plane followed the two-segment path requiring a total flight time of one hour, wind would have pushed the airplane 50 miles east of where the plot in Figure A-1 shows. This is indicated in Figure A-1 with X marking the spot where it actually ends up. Had the plane flown along the diagonal, its flight time would have been 50 minutes, and the wind would have pushed it

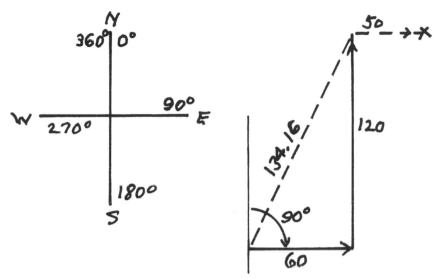

FIGURE A-1.   Air plot for a two-segment flight. Wind effect shown with X.

somewhat less to the right, namely, (50/60) * 50 = 41.67 miles because the wind did not have quite as long a time to push on the airplane.

Important note: In mathematics, vector directions are measured counterclockwise as in Figure A-2*a*. In navigation, angles are measured clockwise from true north to give the "compass rose" as in Figure A-2*b*. The mathematical method is much better if we are dealing with real and complex vectors not related to navigation. The navigation method is quite satisfactory for navigation because "peculiar" numbers do not arise.

The navigator uses a plotting device called the *Weems plotter*, which combines a protractor and a ruler marked in miles (see Figure A-3). Using this, a vector at any specific angle can be plotted. An example: if a plane flies 10 minutes north at 90 degrees, 20 minutes at 120 degrees, and 15 minutes at 180 degrees, all at 180 knots true airspeed, the corresponding distances are 180 * (10/60) = 30, 180 * (20/60) = 60, and 180 * (15/60) = 45 miles. The vector plot of Figure A-4 applies. The total time of flight is 45 minutes, and hence a 40 knot wind from 90 degrees will show that the airplane is

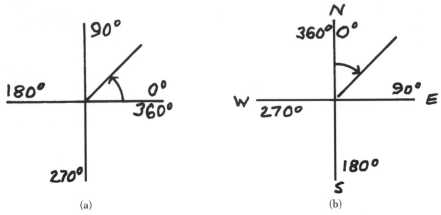

(a)   (b)

FIGURE A-2. Angle measure in mathematics compared with the convention used in navigation.

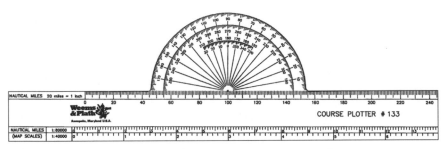

FIGURE A-3. Weems plotter. This is a marine version. Similar to aviation version except that it lacks statute miles scale and has larger mile increments. (Original not available.)

30 miles from the no-wind position. A vector plot can be made of a complete flight without including the wind, with wind included at the very last. This assumes, of course, that the wind has been steady in direction and speed. Up to where the wind is included, the plot is called an *air plot*. The corresponding *ground plot* shows the actual track over the ground. To get the ground plot, the effect of the wind must be shown in each segment of the flight shown in Figure A-4.

In directing an airplane to follow a prescribed path on the ground, the navigator must correct for the wind effect. He or she does this by specifying a compass direction that has the airplane "crabbing" in the wind direction. The air plot will then not go directly to the intended destination. Suppose, for example, that the plane is to have a ground plot due east (90 degrees) for a distance of 240 ground miles at a true air-speed of 180 knots. The wind is 30 knots from a direction of 45 degrees (north-east). How does the navigator proceed? He or she probably uses the E-6B computer, but we show this using vectors directly. Start by drawing the ground path 240 miles long at 90 degrees. The wind is from 45 degrees, but we do not yet know the length of the wind vector because we don't yet know what the duration of the flight will be. Figure A-5 shows the plot along with our dilemma.

The solution to this problem requires that we create a track similar to that of Figure A-5 but of known length. We will assume a flight time of exactly 1 hour, which means that the wind vector will be 30 miles long. Draw this at 45 degrees similarly to the way it was drawn in Figure A-5. The air plot will go

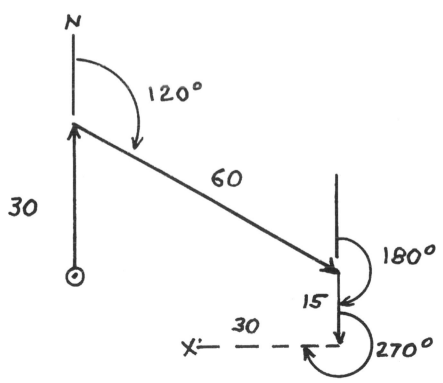

FIGURE A-4.   A three-segment air path made with the plotter.

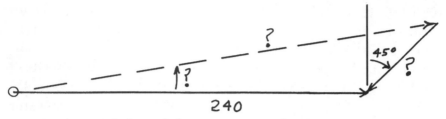

FIGURE A-5. Calculating drift on a one-segment leg.

to the base of the wind vector from the starting point some-where on the ground track. This air plot vector must be 180 miles long because this is the airspeed. Use a compass or a ruler to measure from the base of the wind vector to the ground track with a 180-mile-long line (see Figure A-6). You can now measure the drift angle of 6.5 degrees and the length of the ground vec-tor, which is 167 miles. Tell the pilot to steer a heading that is 6.5 degrees left of the 90 degree course, or 83.5 degrees. The time of flight will be that required to cover 240 miles at a speed of 167 knots, about 1 hour and 26 minutes. The lines and angles of this vector plot solution can all be created using the Weems plotter. The final duration of the flight uses the slide rule part of the E-6B computer to divide 240 by 167 with fractional hours then converted to minutes.

This problem can certainly be solved using various trigono-metric formulas. We do not show any of these here because we have not provided a "course" on the subject of trigonome-try. And besides, the mathematical approach takes too much time in an airplane traveling over hostile territory at a fairly fast clip.

THE E-6B COMPUTER

A variety of other wind triangle problems can be solved using ruler and protractor on the Weems plotter. These include course correction, search patterns, radius of action, intercep-tion, determination of drift angle from bearing measure-ments, and others. Because time is limited in the air and the environment is cumbersome (flight suit, gloves, noise, wind, etc.), the navigator will most likely solve problems using the E-6B computer. It is such an important instrument that we provide a brief theory as to how it can be used for the preceding sample problem. Actually, the E-6B has two sides, one for wind triangle computations and another, which has a circular slide rule and some special windows which we describe later (see Figure A-7).

Think of a track from an origin with 1-hour distance marks corresponding to true airspeed. On this presentation show tracks at various drift angles right and left of the center. Distances from the origin are the same for each track, which requires that these distance lines actually be segments

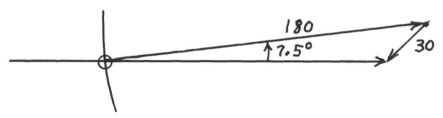

FIGURE A-6.   Example of Figure A-5 for a 1-hour flight.

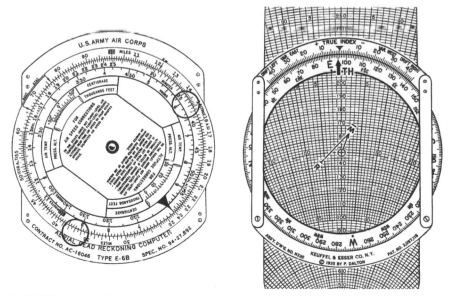

FIGURE A-7.   The two sides of the E-6B computer.

of circles. The bottom part of the display that includes the origin is not included on the plotter because very low speeds are not encountered.

Superimposed on this track and drift card is a compass rose that can be rotated. The rose surrounds a transparent plastic sheet on which vectors can be drawn in pencil. The track card slides up and down under the compass rose. The center of the rose has a hole that is used to place the center of the compass rose over a specific speed value along the center track.

We solve the previous problem for a 1-hour flight time as follows. Set the compass rose at 45 degrees and draw the wind vector from the 45 degree location at the top of the E-6B to the center hole. The circular arcs show distances, and the 30 miles can be drawn using any arcs that are 30 miles apart. Figure A-8 shows this step and also helps to clarify the markings on the computer. The head of the wind arrow rests at the eventual 1-hour destination. This means that the centerline on the slide represents the ground track when the compass rose is rotated to the desired value of 90 degrees. After this rotation, move the slider so that 180 is on the tail of the wind vector as shown in Figure A-9. The radial line at 6.5 degrees represents the air track. Ground speed is read directly at the destination mark with values previously given.

THE COMPASS

The basic instruments for dead reckoning are the compass and the airspeed meter. We discuss various types of compasses here. In discussing the airspeed meter, it will be necessary to also discuss the altimeter and the temperature gauge because these affect readings.

There were four kinds of compasses used in some of our B-24 aircraft: the old-fashioned magnetic compass, the gyrostabilized flux gate compass, the gyrocompass, and the astrocompass. The magnetic and flux gate compasses must be calibrated because the earth's magnetic field can be distorted about the airplane due to the presence of ferromagnetic

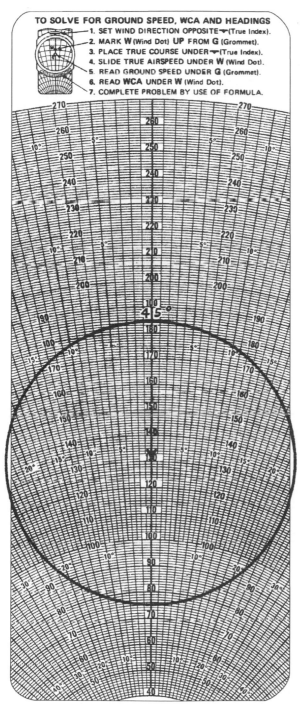

FIGURE A-8. Graphics for the plotting side of the E-6B. The wind of Figure A-6 is shown.

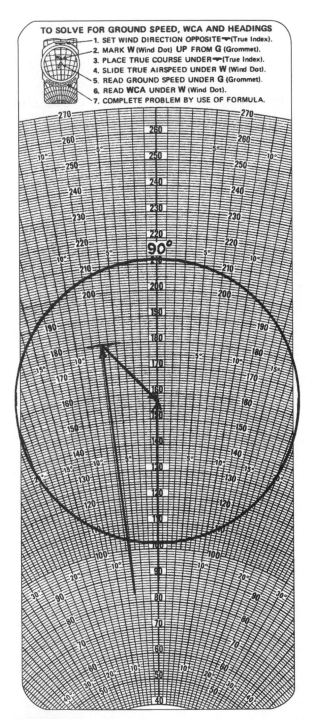

FIGURE A-9. The compass rose of Figure A-8 rotated to 90 degrees with the end of the wind vector on the true airspeed line.

materials (i.e., iron and steel). The frustrating problem with the magnetic compass is its instability in rough air and when turning or banking or changing speed. Some of these problems arise because the earth's magnetic lines of force are not parallel to the surface. Although we used a large compass of the marine type in navigation school, those in B-24s and current general aviation aircraft are not so different from the kinds that are commonly installed in automobiles.

The *flux gate compass* uses a triad of coils that are cycled by currents to a kind of partial saturation that varies depending on the direction of the earth's magnetic field. The coil arrangement is gyrostabilized and placed in a region of the airplane where the effect of stray magnetic fields is relatively small. Gyrostabilization makes its indications much more stable than those from the magnetic compass. Unlike the magnetic compass, the flux gate compass can send its voltages to more than one display.

The *gyrocompass* is basically a spinning top that retains orientation as its housing (the airplane) moves about. Once set, it indicates direction in a stable manner. But it does wobble slightly like a child's top, which is called *precession*. Precession of a satisfactory gyro is slow. The standard during World War II was a limit of 2 or 3 degrees in 15 minutes. Our gyros were spun with a jet of air. Resetting must be done periodically according to the direction given by the magnetic compass.

Yet a fourth kind of compass is the *astrocompass*. This device is meant to track stars and other sky objects such as planets and the sun. Knowing the sidereal time of day and latitude, one can get direction after some computations by sighting a selected object in the sky. A simple example is sighting on the North Star. A compass rose on the instrument can be rotated so that it reads zero degrees when pointed at the North Star. Then the reference line along the axis of the airplane shows the angular heading from true north. This simple method can be as close as can be measured on the scale. *Note:* The North Star is not quite at true north except when it is at either its highest or lowest angle. For any celestial body, with correction for sidereal time, accuracy will be as close as scales on the instrument will permit.

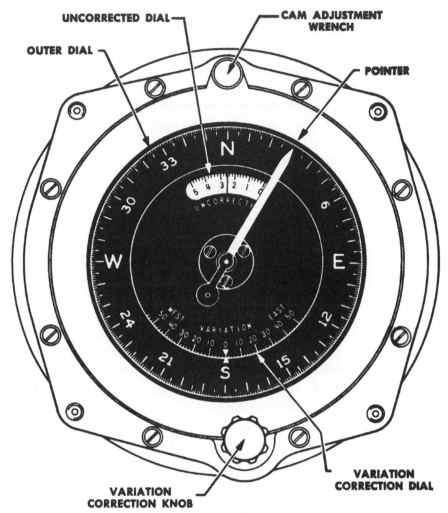

FIGURE A-10.   Face of the gyrostabilized, flux gate compass.

Magnetic north is not the same as true north and can change appreciably during the course of a flight. Finding direction of flight when relatively near to the magnetic north pole can be difficult. The amount by which magnetic north differs from true north is called *magnetic variation*. At my home near Portland, Oregon, the variation is 19 degrees east, which means that a compass points 19 degrees east of true north. Charts meant for air navigation usually show and label lines of constant magnetic variation.

The magnetic or flux gate compass must be calibrated through direct measurement. One way is to align the aircraft in the four cardinal directions and note compass indications. Some compensation is possible with little adjustable magnets, but a residual error will usually remain. Correction numbers are shown on a small card attached directly to the compass, the *compass card*. Some airports have special places where this can be done, usually remote from effects of stray magnetic materials. Marks on the pavement give directions.

Another method uses a calibrated sighting compass held by a person well in front of the airplane with this reading compared to the one in the airplane. Pavement marks are not needed for this. A third method, which can be used in flight, employs the astrocompass, which we have already described.

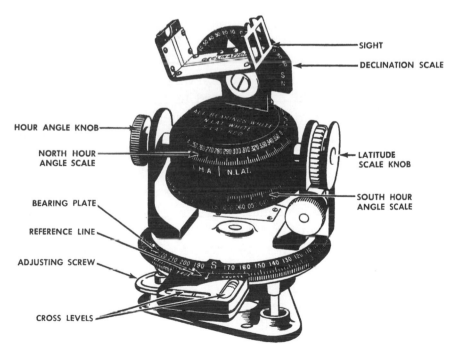

FIGURE A-11. The astrocompass.

MEASURING AIRSPEED AND ALTITUDE

Let's start with the temperature gauge. It appears as a rod that projects from the navigator's window. It does not read the correct temperature. Rather, the friction of air passing by it causes it to be heated slightly. The NIF has a table that shows how much. It is the true airspeed that determines the rise. At 300 knots, the air outside the plane is 9.5 degrees (centigrade) lower than what the meter says. At 100 knots, the reading is high by only 1.1 degrees. Both the altimeter reading and the airspeed reading depend on temperature, via various calculations. It is important to use the correct value in interpreting speed and height.

How do we measure the velocity of the airplane? The airspeed meter says one thing, but this will usually be in error for two reasons. First, the instrument itself may be imperfect and subject to an instrumental error. Second, both altitude and temperature have significant effects. After correcting for instrumental error, true airspeed can be determined, provided that we also have an accurate measure of pressure altitude. A little slide window on the back of the E-6B computer provides the key. Recall, the E-6B is a combination circular slide rule, compass rose, ruler, and plastic marking area upon which vectors may be drawn. It is a standard tool of the navigator and even today remains important if flight paths are to be followed graphically. In fact, the modern E-6B is little different from the one we carried in 1944. There are some minor differences such as a convenient table for converting between the centigrade and Fahrenheit. Otherwise, the device has changed hardly at all over the decades.

But back to the little window. The temperature is found from the thermometer that sticks out of the side window next to the navigator. The value is corrected (an initial adjustment) according to what the airspeed meter reads. The altimeter reads the pressure altitude (provided that the proper barometric pressure has been entered). The altitude value is placed opposite the corrected temperature in the little window. The indicated airspeed corrected for instrument error is located on the inner ring of the slide rule part of the E-6B. Adjacent to this is the true airspeed value. For example, if temperature is −40 degrees and altitude is 20,000 feet, an indicated airspeed of 185 knots yields a true airspeed of 245 knots. Indeed, this correction is extremely important! Note that the original correction of the temperature reading uses a guess as to the true airspeed. Once this is found, then perhaps an airspeed calculation using the corrected value for temperature is warranted because the true airspeed differs from that estimated at the outset.

Getting an accurate measure of altitude is important in finding true airspeed. How is this done? The altimeter is subject to a variety of errors. There is an instrument error, which is best determined by comparing its readings to an accurate barometric pressure reading (on the ground). This requires a special instrument that the navigator does not employ. The altimeter has a knob that changes the setting for barometric pressure. As this knob is rotated, the indicated altitude also changes. If accurate readings are to be obtained, the proper barometric pressure must be set in the instrument. One way to do this is to set the altimeter to read the elevation of the airfield (when on the ground). If there is no instrumentation error, the reading of barometric pressure should agree with that from an accurate instrument. Most likely, however, the navigator sets barometric pressure as provided by the weather bureau. In flight, barometric pressure can change over the flight path. This can introduce errors in what the instrument reads. If radio contact is possible, weather stations along the flight path can give local barometric pressure values that can then be entered into the altimeter. A potentially large error is always present because barometric pressure can change in nonstandard ways as the airplane changes altitude. There is not much that can be done to determine this correction. In a formation, problems are minimized if all planes have altimeters set to the same pressure. Modern high-altitude airliners are required to set altimeters to the normal sea-level pressure of 29.92 inches of mercury. In this way, relative altitudes between aircraft are correctly read, and the danger of collisions is minimized.

But we are not yet done with the altimeter. There is a second little window on the back of the E-6B computer. Place temperature opposite to the pressure altitude. *Pressure altitude* is what the altimeter reads provided that it is set with the correct barometric pressure. The altimeter reading on the inner scale of the slide rule part of the computer is opposite the corrected altimeter value. For example, at a temperature of −40 degrees at a pressure altitude of 20,000 feet, the true altitude is 18,800 feet.

It is important to know that, if the altimeter is not properly set, low-pressure areas can mean that you are lower than the altimeter indicates. This signals danger, especially if you are flying at a low level or taking chances by getting too near to hills and mountains.

Barometric pressure is measured in a basic way by measuring the length of a column of mercury in a tube. The top of the tube is closed, and the space between the top and the mercury is a vacuum. Air pressure at the base of a pool of mercury in which the bottom end of the tube is placed causes the column to rise. The standard reference column height is 29.92 inches at sea level. Weather patterns can cause variations. And certainly the elevation of the mercury barometer is very important. A formula based on a standard lapse rate specifies what the length of the column will be at any particular altitude. At 18,000 feet, for example, it will be about half as tall. But a standard lapse rate is the exception. There will often be upper-level highs or lows so that errors of a kind that cannot easily be corrected are common.

In most of Europe, and increasingly in the United States, barometric pressure is measured in millibars. The standard pressure corresponding to 29.92 inches is 1013.2 millibars. Comparing the two numbers shows that there are approximately 34 millibars to an inch of mercury.

How can the altimeter be calibrated? This is a major shop procedure unless one is fortunate enough to have a radar altimeter. Knowing the height of the ground above sea level and determining the corrected altimeter reading directly indicates whatever error may exist. We had a few radar altimeters but rarely used them. Errors are possible for reasons that may not be familiar such as where exactly the *static port* is placed. The airspeed pick-up is usually a tube sticking out from the front of the wing with a hole at the end that is subject to "ram" pressure. This pressure is compared to "static" pressure in order to move the bellows in the altimeter and then the indicating needle. Clearly, any unusual air motions around the static port can lead to inaccurate results. It is not proper to use cabin pressure for this because it may differ significantly from the true static pressure. Location of the static port is also important to altimeter readings. It is quite possible that a compression effect can result in the measured static pressure at the static port being different from the "true" static pressure, depending on airspeed. The navigator does not have the ability to make changes in the location of the static port but can only try to compensate for errors, report problems to the instrument shop, and so on. A suspected error in either instrument might call for clearing out the tubes leading to the static port (but do so blowing outward so as to avoid damaging instruments).

The window for airspeed correction also gives density altitude. Density altitude indicates how well the aircraft will climb or how short will be its takeoff run. On a hot day, density altitude can be considerably higher than actual altitude. This condition has led to many accidents when small aircraft try to take off from airports in the high country. *Example:* At 40 degrees centigrade (104 degrees Fahrenheit), an airport at 7000 feet above sea level will have a density altitude of 11,000 feet!

How can we calibrate the airspeed meter so as to determine instrument error? Find a region having two well-defined parallel lines some distance apart, perhaps 5 minutes of flight time. Avoid testing if wind speed is high. Fly between lines in both directions with the airplane headed perfectly perpendicular to the lines. Don't correct for drift and keep the aircraft headed as if there were no drift. The lines must be clearly observed on the ground, and the distance between them must be known to the same accuracy as we want to obtain for instrument readings. Time the flight time between lines in each direction. The average of these two times is the time that would be required in still air. The navigator carried a stop-watch for measuring critical time intervals. Use the time-distance formula to calculate the average speed (using the slide rule on the E-6B computer), and compare the result with what the instrument indicates after correcting for true airspeed.

If wind speed is known and/or its direction is abeam the aircraft, and if wind speed is not too great, a reasonably accurate estimate can be made by first calculating ground speed. This can be done by timing a flight between any two well-marked and mapped points on the ground. It is possible that one or both of the references can be had from radio bearings or Loran or other (as discussed later).

DRIFT METER

Another important instrument is the *drift meter*. One cannot always depend on predicted wind speeds and directions. Being able to measure the wind effect can greatly improve precision in navigation. Several tools for doing this are available. But only one permits values to be obtained through single measurements without geographical reference marks. This tool is the drift meter. Its main disadvantage is that the ground or sea surface must be visible. Imagine a lens with a thin line marked in the direction of the front-rear axis of the airplane. This line can be rotated slightly. In zero wind, an object on the ground will follow this line if it is set at zero angle with respect to the axis of the airplane. But if the wind is pushing the plane sideways, an object on the ground will not track the line unless the line is suitably rotated. The angle of rotation is the *drift angle*. In bumpy weather, it can be quite difficult to get a good drift reading with an older-style meter such as the Model B-5. A superior instrument, Model B-3, has the lens that carries the line stabilized with a gyroscope, and with it bouncing about has a much reduced effect. I used both types. But I certainly prefer the gyro unit!

The drift meter also has lines at the extreme ends of the lens that are perpendicular to the axial line. If one knows the altitude above ground, then the time for an object on the ground to move from one extreme line to the other can be used to compute ground speed. If one can get both ground speed and drift angle, and knowing the airspeed, then wind speed and direction can be calculated. Over the ocean, drift readings are still possible provided that there is a reasonable number of white caps. Of course, if the ground is obscured by clouds, fog, or smoke, the drift meter is useless. The Norden bombsight is also a good drift meter.

A special computer was installed in some of the aircraft. It was called an *air position indicator*. It would take data from the compass and the airspeed meter and plot the movement of the airplane using these data. This was done in an ingenious manner. The diaphragm in a special airspeed meter moves according to the difference in pressure between the pitot tube and static pressures. A little fan in the device would keep the diaphragm at a constant reference position by turning on and off. The fan motor was geared to a shaft that would move the marking pen. The place where the pen moved was rotated according to data from the flux gate compass. Some general aviation aircraft are currently equipped with such a device, but now, of course, everything is solid state and microprocessors. (I didn't have an air position indicator in my B-24.)

OTHER AIDS TO NAVIGATION

So far we have discussed only those tools that permit air plots with wind corrections from weather data or using a drift meter. There are other ways to determine drift and ground speed. And there are several ways to get a fix. We will discuss several instruments here but not in the detail presented before.

The basic tool for doing celestial navigation is the *bubble sextant*. This device has only one function, namely, to find the angle above the horizon of a star, planet, the sun, etc. A marking device on a disk would put down a mark every second or so for a period of perhaps 30 seconds while the navigator continued to track the star or sun by holding the image in the

FIGURE A-12.   The B-3 gyrostabilized drift meter in use.

center of a bubble. The bubble was nothing more than a leveling device so that the sextant would be held horizontal to the earth in both directions (forward-backward and side to side). The navigator manually pushed a marking pencil on a disk for Model A-10. An electric solenoid replaced the manual process in type A-10A. I used the A-10. The several marks would be visually averaged, and the time would be that corresponding to the middle of the observation time. It is important to note that one-sixtieth of a degree error can be about 1 nautical mile of error. And a time error of 4 seconds can be a distance error of about a mile. After making a measurement and doing some calculating with special star charts and tables, one comes up with a *line of position*. The plane was on this line at the (middle) time the measurements were made. A second measurement some time later gives a second line of position at a second time. The distance between these lines relative to the time difference gives the ground speed.

The simplest way of understanding this uses the North Star. Take a sextant reading at time 1 and a second one at time 2, both close enough in time so that the North Star does

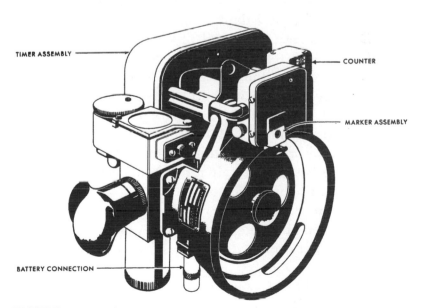

FIGURE A-13.   The A-10A sextant with automatic marker.

not rotate about true north by an appreciable amount. The difference in the two angles is the distance in nautical miles.

Another method for getting ground speed is to make sightings on an object on the ground. One might use a mountain or a bend in a river or a shoreline or some other identifiable feature. Take two bearings at spaced time intervals. Use the astrocompass for this (with the declination set to zero). If you know the distance to the object, ground speed can be calculated. Actually, if this distance is known, you have also obtained a fix—that is, you know where you are.

A similar method of taking bearings can be used with the radio compass. How does a *radio compass* work? If you have a small pocket AM radio, tune in to a station that is not too strong and hold the radio horizontally. Rotate it to find where the signal fades away to substantially zero. There is a little "loopstick" antenna in the radio. The null occurs when the stick is oriented to point directly at the radio station (as well as directly away). The null can be quite sharp so that, if the radio is mounted on a compass rose, you can get an accurate measure of angle. Do this a second time for a second angle and, if you know distance to the radio, you can get ground speed as well as a fix. Our radio direction finders did not use ferrite loopsticks because I don't believe ferrite materials had yet been invented. We used a coil of wire about 8 inches in diameter housed in a teardrop-shaped device usually placed above the main cabin of the plane. The loop inside could be rotated via an electrical motor or, in some cases, directly with a flexible shaft. A special switch setting would indicate if the station was in front or in back. Radio direction finding can be done on a standard broadcast radio station. But a special system of stations exists for aircraft radio, and these operate at frequencies below the broadcast band.

The radio compass direction can be in error if the radio waves have bounced off of mountains or have been affected by marked differences in terrain. The error can be several degrees.

Another method for getting ground speed, somewhat similar to that using a sextant, employs the *Loran receiver*. This system works by having two well-spaced transmitters send out

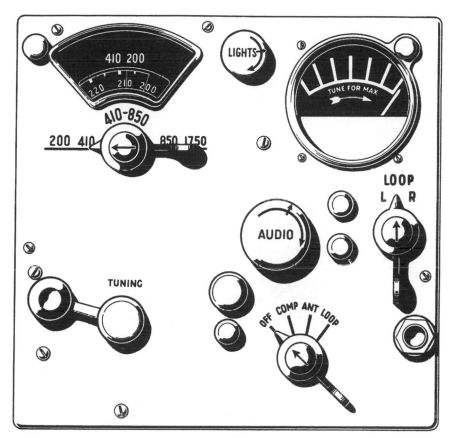

FIGURE A-14.   Control panel of the radio compass.

pulses that are accurately separated in time with both stations at the same frequency. A receiver in the airplane would pick up both pulses and show them on an oscilloscope screen as blips above a line. With knobs and switches, we would measure the time delay between the two pulses, down to a microsecond. A special map showed the locations of the two transmitters and a series of lines of position along which time of arrival differences were constant. We would go to the appropriate line (a hyperbola) and know we were somewhere on this line. After a few minutes we could take another measurement to get a second line. If we knew approximately where we were, the distance between lines and the two times could be used to determine a ground speed. Lines of equal time differences are not separated by equal distances along their routes, and so an error could occur if we didn't know approximately where we were.

During World War II, Loran transmitters operated at frequencies just above the standard broadcast band. One of the peculiarities of radio propagation at these frequencies is that range is limited during the daylight but can be very great at night when the charged ionosphere reflects the radio signals

RADIO SET AN/APN-4 AND RADAR SET AN/APN-9

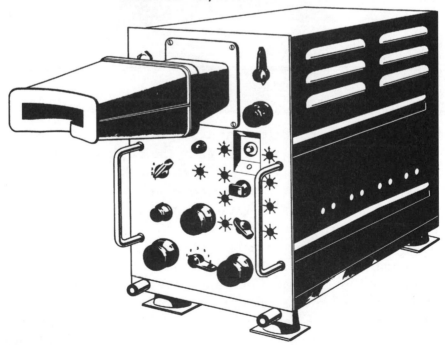

FIGURE A-15.   Loran receiver.

back to earth. When such reflections occur, errors will occur because the distance traveled by the radio waves is not the same as distance along the ground, and distance traveled by each of the two pulses may be affected differently. But errors were not likely to be serious enough to endanger long overwater flights.

Modern Loran receivers now operate at frequencies below the broadcast band, and even below frequencies used in radio direction finders. As a result, Loran can have a quite long range without errors due to the ionosphere.

GETTING FIXES

We have already suggested methods that, with minor extensions, can lead to a fix. First, of course, is finding where you are over the ground by visual means. This is called *pilotage*. The item might be a lake or a particular bend in a river or a railroad bridge or a city or almost any other identifiable point. If you know your altitude, and if you can estimate the dip angle to the object on the ground, then you can figure the distance that you are to one side. If you can take bearings on two prominent objects and if you know from the map how far apart these two objects are, then you can get a fix in a straightforward manner. The triangle that results from this measurement has its base known (distance between objects) and both angles at the base. If you time yourself between two fixes and you know your true airspeed, then you can compute wind speed and direction.

A Loran or a celestial "shot" gives you a line of position. To get a fix, make a measurement with a second Loran station or a second celestial shot to get a second line of position. You can even mix celestial and Loran lines. If properly selected, the two lines intersect at a reasonably large angle. You are at this point. Note, however, that the two lines are not obtained at the same time. The first line must be moved up according to your dead-reckoning distance to the time of the second line. By then you have flown beyond the second line, but at least you have a new starting point. If possible, especially with celestial measurements, you might try to get three lines of position that intersect to form a small triangle. Your estimate of location is the middle of the triangle.

The radio compass can also be used to get a fix. You need to have two stations, and you must know the distance between them, much the same as using visual means with two objects on the ground.

A special navigational method where one line of position can suffice is called a *landfall*. You fly to one side of the destination and choose a *line of position* (LOP) that goes through the destination approximately perpendicular to your line of flight. When you reach this LOP, turn to the destination in the same direction as the LOP. Just be careful. If you want a small island and you are right of it instead of left where you thought you were, you will fly into never-never land.

We have not yet mentioned an important consideration in using celestial navigation. Over the years, the positions of stars relative to one another remain unchanged for all practical purposes. But not so relative to us on earth. The earth is like a spinning top and has precession. What we call the North Star today will not be the North Star in a couple of thousand years. The angle we measure to the North Star (or any other star because these all measure accurately from the North Star) will change by about 1.4 degrees per century. One degree of angle to the North Star is 60 minutes of arc or 60 nautical miles. A change of 1.4 degrees can turn into an error of $1.4 * 60 = 84$ miles! It has been over a half century since I navigated in World War II. An error of 42 miles could result using star tables dating from that period. *Be advised*: If you want to do celestial navigation, have appropriate tables, and know how to correct for the time interval between the date the tables were made and your current date.

If one could measure the angle of the North Star for 24 hours, it would follow a full circle about true north. The average of maximum and minimum elevation angles will be the true latitude. (There could be a small correction for diffraction as starlight gets slightly bent in coming through the earth's atmosphere at an angle.) Other stars not too far from true north can be used in such a calculation as well. If you know how the North Star lines up with some other stars, such as part of the Big Dipper, a fairly good estimate for the correction to the reading that you make with the sextant can be had. If you can follow the North Star for a few hours and get sufficiently accurate readings, you might be able to complete the circle represented by the arc that you measured.

WHAT IS NAVIGATION LIKE TODAY?

Shortly after the war, the network of low-frequency radio stations became available to all suitably equipped aircraft, and panel-mounted radios with needles that pointed to a radio station could be obtained. The more important system was the *vector omnirange* (VOR). It operates at ultrahigh frequencies, between low and high television bands. With this you can get a bearing without having to rotate a loop antenna. A system of airways was set up with many VOR transmitters so that you could fly between cities and airports by simply following the needle. A somewhat later embellishment, mostly for military aircraft, was the addition of a beacon system so that range to the VOR transmitter could also be obtained. Another augmentation made the system suitable for use in instrument landings. One could, and still can, get battery-powered communications transmitter-receivers with built-in VOR for only a few hundred dollars.

Somewhat later, the Loran system was redesigned to use very low frequencies. This greatly improved its accuracy and reliability. Hand-held Loran receivers then became available. With three or four Loran transmitters, it becomes possible to get a fix rather than just a line of position. A built-in computer could then show you your coordinates. These could be superimposed on a map of the area that showed towns, cities, navigational aids, airports, and so on.

The most recent development is the satellite navigation system called the *ground position system* (GPS). This uses 24 satellites in near-earth orbit. It is becoming possible to locate yourself to within a few feet, not only on a map but even your altitude! Such an aid will soon be legalized for instrument landing approaches, making the current *instrument landing system* (ILS) unnecessary.

The Federal Aviation Administration (FAA) plans to phase out all current navigational systems except for GPS. The present GPS became operational only in 1995. Beginning in 2005, older systems will gradually be decommissioned, and all will be removed by the year 2010. This is only a dozen years from now!

The GPS used in aircraft, costing from under $500 to about $2500 (for general aviation aircraft), can have all of the "bells and whistles" needed to navigate without worry or concern or even without much training. If the pilot is worried about reliability, then simply have a back-up GPS receiver or perhaps two back-ups. Because GPS gives altitude to within a few feet, an altimeter is not really needed any more. The GPS can take location differences continuously and show this in the form of ground speed, distance, heading, and time to the next checkpoint or destination, and on and on.

The GPS is also finding its way into civilian automobiles, boats, and even the pockets of hikers and backpackers. A recent ad from a discount department store shows a small hand-held battery-powered unit for under $150. For a few dollars extra per day, you can rent a car equipped with GPS.

The navigator is a relic, like the Wells Fargo stagecoach driver or wagon master. What this means is that our training as navigators was a "bust" in terms of preparing us for reentry into the labor force. Pilots could find new jobs. Only the bombardier fell below us navigators in the futility of our training for future employment. There was a short period following the war where classical navigators were needed, but this ended with the Korean conflict in the early 1950s. We did get useful training of an academic kind, which, at least for me, paid off in speeding my reentry to civilian life and education toward an engineering degree.

During the war over Germany, all of the electronic navigation aids were thoroughly jammed. This implies that the modern devices could also be jammed. But could we ever again have a war involving lumbering daylight bombers? Not unless we want to intervene between tribes somewhere in the middle of the Amazon jungle!

But what if we do have another big war? I think it will have to be a "gentlemanly" war without use of nuclear, chemical, or biological weapons. The fear of retaliation might keep combatants from using these terrible weapons. Such a war might reduce to shooting missiles at one another, using conventional warheads. With antimissile missiles and laser weapons, we would seek to not only destroy incoming missiles but also the satellites used to guide these missiles as well as submarines and aircraft that are invisible to radar. The winner of a conflict could be the side that can keep the most satellites in orbit. But victory must also be "gentlemanly" else the loser will be tempted to use some horrible weapon in a last attempt to preserve independence.

This of course is only one possible scenario out of many and may be quite unlikely. But it does point out one thing. If all of the satellites are destroyed, how do we navigate? Recall, the FAA plans to dismantle all other systems, and so there will no longer be a backup.

A LITTLE ALGEBRA

Computations for time and distance can be made graphically with a vector plot. Let's pause to carefully define a *vector* for the benefit of those who have not played with such things for years. Add 2 and 3. Define a vector 2 and another one 3. Add the 3 to the 2 in a tail-to-head fashion to get the resulting vector 5 as in Figure A-16a. If we add $3 + 2$ instead of $2 + 3$, we obviously get the same result, as in Figure A-16b. This property is called the *commutative law of addition*: If a and b are numbers, then $a + b = b + a$.

In algebra, we can work with both real and imaginary (and complex) numbers. We won't discuss the imaginary kind. For the needs of basic theory, we must define operations with real numbers. That the sum of two real numbers is a real number

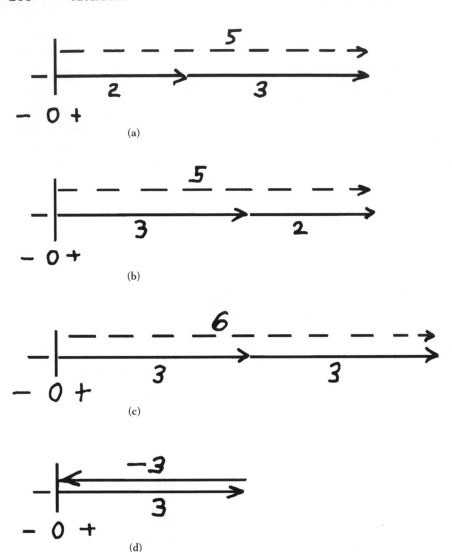

FIGURE A-16.   Vector addition in (a) and (b). Multiplication in (c). Additive inverse in (d).

is called the *closure law of addition*. A similar *closure law of multiplication* means that the product of two real numbers is a real number.

If we add 2 vectors of 3 units each, we can say 3 + 3 = 6 or use the multiplication symbol instead as 2 * 3 = 6 (see Figure A-16c). We get the same results with 3 vectors of 2 units each. That 2 * 3 = 3 * 2 is called the *commutative law of multiplica-*

tion. That is, if a and b are numbers, then $a * b = b * a$. If we have 3 vectors 2, 3, and 4, the sum is 9. We get the same result by creating a single vector 2 + 3 and adding it to 4, or a single vector 2 + 4 added to 3, and so on. This is called the *associative law of addition*. In terms of letters representing numbers, $a + b + c = (a + b) + c = (a + c) + b$, and so on. The *associative law of multiplication* applies when 3 numbers are multiplied because the order of multiplication can be changed: $2 * 3 * 4 = 4 * 2 * 3$, etc. In letters, $a * b * c = b * a * c$. Or we can combine to find $(a * b) * c = d * c$ if $d = a * b$.

A real number can be either positive or negative. Negative numbers are shown with vectors that point in the opposite direction from those representing positive numbers. A special case of this is called the *additive inverse*. This is when a positive number and a negative one of equal value add to zero (see Figure A-16d). The *multiplicative inverse* says that a number divided by the same number has a value of 1. That is, $7/7 = 1$, or $a/a = 1$.

A few more virtually obvious laws and we will be finished with this excursion into algebra. The *zero law* is $5 * 0 = 0$. The *additive identity* is $6 + 0 = 6$. The *multiplicative identity* is $8 * 1 = 8$. The *distributive law for multiplication* allows one to put numbers into subgroups. It's simpler than it sounds. For example, $3(1 - 2) = 3 * 1 - 3 * 2 = -3$. Note that we do not have to use the * symbol between the 3 and the first parenthesis because it is implied. We can certainly show this if there is any possibility for confusion. We can go beyond this with two products as $(2 + 3) * (4 - 7) = 2 * 4 - 2 * 7 + 3 * 4 - 3 * 7 = -15$. Or we would do this in smaller steps as $2(4 - 7) + 3(4 - 7)$.

In all of these manipulations, we have used ordinary integer numbers. Clearly, these could be fractional or decimal numbers. We may frequently represent numbers with letters. For example, $a(b + c) = d$ can have $a = 2$, $b = 3$, $c = 4$ to give $d = 14$.

Congratulations. You have just learned most of the fundamental algebraic laws. It's pretty obvious when you interpret numbers as simple right-pointing or left-pointing vectors.

These laws extend to the time-distance equation $d = v * t$ where d = distance, v = velocity, and t = time. If we do exactly the same thing to both sides of an equation, the equals sign is not changed. From $d = v * t$, divide both sides by t. Then note that we can write the result as a product of two parts with one part being equal to unity by virtue of the multiplicative inverse law. Specifically:

$$d = v * t \quad d/t = v * t/t \quad \text{thus} \quad v = d/t$$

The reader can find the formula for t in a similar manner.

The rule to do the same thing to both sides of an equation is quite general if we want the result to remain an equality. We can add the same number (or symbol) to both sides, divide or multiply by the same number, raise both sides to the same power or root, and so on. Do only one thing at a time and you won't get into any trouble. Just be sure that what you do applies to the complete left or right side of the equation. The same rules apply when using greater than or less than symbols. That is, if $a + b > c + d$, then doing the same thing to both sides will not invalidate the inequality sign.

A common task in arithmetic is to add two fractions or change a mixed number into a single fraction. Examples:

$$\text{Mixed fraction:} \quad 3\frac{1}{2} = 3 + \frac{1}{2} = \frac{3 * 2}{1 * 2} + \frac{1}{2} = \frac{6}{2} + \frac{1}{2} = \frac{7}{2}$$

$$\text{Sum of fractions:} \quad \frac{2}{3} + \frac{3}{4} = \frac{2 * 4}{3 * 4} + \frac{3 * 3}{4 * 3}$$

$$= \frac{8}{12} + \frac{9}{12} = \frac{17}{12}$$

In the second example, a shorthand method can be applied. Cross multiply numerator and denominator, and add the two products to get the numerator of the result, and multiply both denominators to get the new denominator. (*Recall terms*: When in the form of a fraction, the numerator is divided by the denominator.)

$$\text{Cross multiplication:} \quad \frac{8}{9} + \frac{1}{3} = \frac{8 * 3 + 1 * 9}{9 * 3} =$$

$$\frac{24 + 9}{27} = \frac{33}{27}$$

The concept of the *lowest common denominator* (LCD) can be demonstrated with a simple example. The object is to divide the numerator and denominator by the same number, perhaps again and again, until the numerator and the denominator no longer have a common multiplier. We use the result of the cross multiplication example above:

$$\text{LCD:} \quad \frac{33}{27} = \frac{\dfrac{33}{3}}{\dfrac{27}{3}} = \frac{11}{9}$$

Note: It is usually not necessary to reduce a fraction to its lowest common denominator form when calculated results are desired. With a low-cost pocket calculator or with a slide rule, finding $^{33}/_{27}$ is no more difficult than finding $^{11}/_{9}$.

A word of caution: Vectors described here can be multiplied or divided by ordinary numbers—not by other vectors. One can multiply and divide two phasors, which are like vectors but refer to the complex plane. The formal vector calculus does not define division of one vector by another, and multiplication of one by another gives quite different results called dot products and cross products. These other kinds of vectors are not considered here.

SOURCES OF INFORMATION

VETERANS GROUPS

The number of stories, articles, and books relating to the air war of World War II is virtually uncountable. I have limited references in this appendix to those that were used directly in preparing this book.

The Pearson Airfield in Vancouver, Washington, boasts a very nice "Pearson Air Museum." In 1994 there was a grand reopening of the museum and dedication of the B-24 exhibit. Residents of Vancouver, Clark County, and surrounding areas who flew in B-24s or had much to do with these were featured in the B-24 display (including the author). The display was the almost-single-handed work of Bruce Barker, son of a World War II soldier (ground troops). When I decided to make progress on this book, I contacted Mr. Barker who provided me with considerable information and miscellaneous publications. Most important of these were copies of the Second Air Division newsletters. I was not aware of the existence of this association of World War II flyers and ground personnel that made up the Second Air Division.

Second Air Division Association Journal
Neal Sorensen, President
132 Peninsula Road
Medicine Lake, MN 55441
Ray Pytel, Editor
Post Office Box 484
Elkhorn, WI 53121

But there is more. Another regular newsletter features my own old group with a regular short report appearing in the *Second Air Division Journal*:

Poop from Group 467
Walter J. Mundy, President
24030 Basin Harbor Court
Tehachapi, CA 93561

As you might suspect by now, the 8th Air Force, with two divisions of B-17s and one of B-24s, has a newsletter:

8th AF News
Huburt M. Childress, President
48988 Sunny Summit Lane
Palm Desert, CA 92260

I don't have information relating to other air force veterans' organizations such as the 12th in Africa, 15th in Italy, or those in the Pacific theater. The ubiquitous B-24 was everywhere! I suspect that most World War II flyers tried to keep together by forming a variety of associations.

Mr. Barker provided a useful history book of a most readable kind that got into some of the guiding philosophy of the generals that ran the air war:

The Air War in Europe
Ronald H. Bailey
Time-Life Books, Inc.
Alexandria, VA

In addition to making up the display and making available considerable material, Mr. Barker wrote his own book, but

printed it only for those with local interests: *B24 Liberator &
WWII Airmen of Clark County.*

I have often referred to Allan Healy's book, which has been
an important and major reference for me:

*The 467th Bombardment Group,
September 1943 to June, 1945*

This was privately published in 1947. In his preface, Mr.
Healy credits all photographs to the group, either on operational
missions or by the Photo Section at the base. The book has been
reprinted more than once. The last, fourth time, was in 1993 by
467th Book Group, 8570 North Mulberry Drive, Tucson, AZ
85704. This last printing contained a more complete list of
names and casualties as well as a discussion of the preparation
for a mission by Col. Shower, the 467th Commanding Officer.

DAVID DAVIS

One of the issues of the *Second Air Division Newsletter* (Fall,
1992) had an article on David Davis and his wing. The author,
Allen G. Blue, must have had a copy of the original report
because he gives the same quote as I have presented in
Chapter 12. Mr. Blue's article was not technical enough to
satisfy me. But it did point to the place where original wind
tunnel tests were carried out. So I wrote for information. Not
only did I get a copy of the original report but I even got
copies of letters agreeing to make the tests. My benefactor
could not have been better placed; and he is also involved with
aircraft historical societies:

Charles Landry, Ph.D.
Manager, GALCIT Subsonic Wind Tunnels
California Institute of Technology
1201 East California Boulevard
Pasadena, CA 91125

The report I received is:

Wind Tunnel Tests on a Davis Tapered
Monoplane Wind and a Similar
Consolidated Corporation Wing (September 13, 1937).
Clark B. Millikan
Guggenheim Aeronautical Laboratory
California Institute of Technology
Pasadena, CA

(You should be able to identify what GALCIT stands for.) Mr. Davis cooperated with the Consolidated Corporation, which covered the costs of testing. The B-24 was later designed by Consolidated Corporation with volume production by them, Ford Motor Co., and others.

There is much more that can be said about David Davis and his wing. He developed his designs using mathematics that do not directly relate to modern aerodynamic theory. In fact, neither he nor those in related engineering fields really could correlate his form of mathematical analysis to experimental data. The technology at the time, in the 1930s, was not as sophisticated as it became when the war effort demanded better correspondence between theory and practice. As later became evident, the Davis wing was really no more efficient than some of the earlier NACA designs when these were configured to a similar aspect ratio with taper. As a result, Davis occupies only a small niche in aerodynamic theory and his wing is no longer held as a model of unusual efficiency. Apparently its advantages diminished as airspeeds crept upward toward those that characterize modern airliners. Perhaps Davis was like the medical doctor who created a useful treatment but for the wrong (theoretical) reasons. Nevertheless, David Davis and his wing form a central binding identification with B-24 crewmembers.

Davis received two patents, the second one being different primarily in terms of the details of the mathematics that he offered:

David Davis, Fluid Foil, patent number 1,942,688, application date May 25, 1931, issued January 9, 1934.

David Davis, Fluid Foil, patent number 2,281,272, application date May 9, 1938, issued April 28, 1942.

A most interesting study of Davis and the general relationship between theory and experiment as a technology matures is:

Walter G. Vincenti, "The Davis Wing and the Problem of Airfoil Design: Uncertainty and Growth in Engineering Knowledge," *Technology and Culture*, vol. 27, no. 4 (October, 1986). Society for the History of Technology.

For those with the necessary technical and mathematical background, I cite two books on aerodynamics and wings. One is very old and probably out of print. The other might still be available. Our airplanes and wings fit into the "old" category and are best referenced with "old" concepts having nothing to do with computers.

Elliott G. Reid, *Applied Wing Theory*

(Stanford, Calif. Stanford University, Division of Aeronautical Engineering, 1932) (Reprinted at least through 1958).

Ira H. Abbot and Albert E. Von Doenhoff, *Theory of Wing Sections*

(New York: Dover Publications, 1949) (Dover edition 1958).

FAMOUS NAMES

The recent death of actor Jimmy Stewart (no relation) gives reason to identify him with B-24s. He was Group Operations Officer of the 445th Bomb Group of the Second Air Division. He flew 20 missions as a command pilot or observer and reached the rank of colonel when in England. The town of Indiana, Pennsylvania, has for several years had a Jimmy Stewart Museum. It is likely that interest in this museum will increase now that Jimmy is dead.

Walter Mathau was a radio operator and gunner in the 453rd Bomb Group.

Joseph Kennedy, Jack's older brother, flew B-24s of the Second Division on some special missions. The air force wanted to destroy submarine pens, which were protected by concrete domes up to 30 feet thick. A secret mission was created, called "Operation Aprodites." The idea was to load a B-24 with 20,000 pounds of explosives and guide it by remote control from a nearby airplane to its target. The bomber had to be controlled by a human until near enemy lines, at which time the pilot would bail out with a special unit sent to pick him up. Kennedy was killed when his load of explosives blew up prematurely, before he was scheduled to bail out.

Our B-24 friends in Italy included some well-known names. George McGovern and Lloyd Bentsen were pilots.

Year	Age	Left
1993	70	8000
1997	74	6800
2000	77	5957
2003	80	4636
2008	85	2732
2017	90.3	1366

HOW LONG CAN WE LAST?

Ray Pytel, in the *Second Division Newsletter*, gives a table based on statistics (available through HEW) of how long a white male will live once he has achieved a certain age. (I don't recall any flight personnel who was not a white male.) The assumption is that, in 1993, the average age was 70 (both air and ground personnel). He assumes a total of 8000 467th personnel left in 1993 and tracks year by year how many will be left.

We have a few years left. In part, our legacy must provide a true rendition of what we did and how we did it. The passage of time all too often muddles reality by implanting preconceived notions and biases generated by those with no direct experience. A recent example has been the treatment of the *Enola Gay* and the atom bombing of Japan put forth by the Smithsonian Institution. Pressure from us old guys has had some effect in correcting a lopsided picture of our thoughts and concepts of moral values.

THE REUNION OF 1992

The Yanks of the Army Air Corps first arrived in England in 1942. The year 1992 marked the 50th anniversary. An impressive celebration resulted. The British continue to show gratitude and affection for us Yanks. There are numerous active air museums including a library in Norwich dedicated to the Second Air Division. The map of Figure 6-1 is from a brochure inviting Yanks to come and visit.

The folks in East Anglia and Norwich continue to welcome us old vet flyers. Their museums and libraries remain open. There even exists a special commemorative monument for the 467th.

Sir Henry no longer occupies his cottage, which has fallen into a state of some disrepair. But an effort is underway to restore it for conversion to seven luxury flats (apartments). Nobility in England lost a lot of their clout and income after the war with taxes digging ever deeper into pocketbooks. Ability to hire servants and pay taxes forced many to abandon their mansions and relocate to smaller quarters.

PEARSON AIRFIELD

Not many people appreciate the historical importance of Vancouver's own Pearson Airfield. It is located contiguous with Fort Vancouver, which was originally established by the Hudson Bay Trading Company. Previous to this, the Lewis and Clark Expedition in the early 1800s explored the area. The Vancouver community is considered to be the oldest (non-Native American) settlement in the Northwest.

Pearson Airpark (recently changed to "Pearson Airfield") is the oldest operating airfield in the United States dating to a dirigible landing in 1905. Lincoln Beachy piloted the dirigible, *Gelatine*, on this flight, which was also the first aerial crossing of the Columbia River. The first airplane flight was in 1911 at what was then known as the "polo grounds" of Vancouver Barracks. Through ensuing years the site continued to be a favorite of experimental aviators in the Northwest.

The army built and operated a cut-up mill on the field to produce airplane lumber (spruce) for Allied plane-building efforts during World War I. Flying by the Army Air Service began in 1921 when a forest patrol base was established here. Reserve fliers from the region trained with the 321st Observation Squadron from 1923 until 1941 when the unit was put on active duty. Lt. Oakley Kelly who, along with Lt. John Macready, made the first nonstop transcontinental flight (1923), commanded the 321st from 1924 through 1928. Kelly was instrumental in establishing the adjacent commercial field (1925). The military and commercial fields were later joined to form Pearson Airpark. The commercial portion of Pearson Field was a stop on the original West Coast airmail route. Pacific Air Transport and Varney Airlines both used the field. These companies later joined with two others to form United Airlines.

Lt. Alexander Pearson attended high school in Vancouver. Among his accomplishments was winning the speed contest in the first cross-country flying race. Pearson bested 73 other pilots in the 1919 event, which stretched from New York to San Francisco and back, in 48 hours, 14 minutes, and 8 seconds of flying time. In recognition of his flying skills, the Department of the Interior commissioned him to make the first aerial survey of the Grand Canyon. He was one of three army pilots selected for the 1924 Pulitzer Races. Pearson was killed when the wings of his plane collapsed during a practice run. The army honored him in 1925 by naming the field for him.

Pearson Field was used and visited by a number of leading aviators. Tex Rankin had a flying operation on the field at various times. Other visitors included Charles Lindbergh, Jimmy Doolittle, Eddie Rickenbacker, and T. Claude Ryan. Pearson was the last stopover of the army's epochal Round-the-World flight of 1924. Five years later, the *Land of the Soviets* touched down. On June 20, 1937, the entire world focused on Pearson Field when the first nonstop transpolar flight landed here. The huge ANT-25 monoplane had flown from Moscow, USSR, in 63 hours, 16 minutes. A stone memorial at Pearson Airfield commemorates the event. It may be the only Russian memorial in the nation. The transpolar flight remains one of the most important marks of achievement for Russians, rather like our recognition of Lindbergh.